NATIVE GRANDEUR

Preserving California's Vanishing Landscapes

NATIVE GRANDEUR

Preserving California's Vanishing Landscapes

by DAVID WICINAS

with
JOAN IRVINE SMITH
JEAN STERN
E.O. WILSON
DONN MILLER
and
HEATHER TRIM
JIM MOORE
MARTIN GRIFFIN
JULES EVENS
JULIE PACKARD
DIANA LINDSAY

SCOTT LeFEVRE
ALICIA SANDERSON
NICHOLAS CHICKERING
MARY NICHOLS
JOHN DOFFLEMYER
ROBIN WILLS
TUPPER ANSEL BLAKE
ZENAIDA MOTT
PAUL McHUGH
GORDON HULL
KEVIN STARR

Edited by LOUISA HUFSTADER

Executive Editors:
JENNIFER CALDWELL and
MARK SANDERSON
with FRYAR CALHOUN

The Nature Conservancy
CALIFORNIA

A Publication of the Nature Conservancy of California

Native Grandeur: Preserving California's Vanishing
Landscapes/ by David Wicinas et.al. —1st. ed.

ISBN 0-9624590-5-4
Library of Congress Card Number: 00-107451
Printed in Italy

Front Cover Painting:
HANSON PUTHUFF (1875-1972)
Mystical Hills
oil on canvas, 26 x 34 inches
The Irvine Museum

Back Cover Painting:
EUGEN NEUHAUS (1879-1963)
Mouth of the Navarro, Mendocino, California
tempera on canvas, 24-1/8 x 20-1/8 inches
Courtesy of the Garzoli Gallery, San Rafael

Book design: DENNIS GALLAGHER, JOHN SULLIVAN
Visual Strategies/visdesign.com

The Nature Conservancy of California
201 Mission Street, 4th Floor
San Francisco, California 94105
415-777-0487
www.tnccalifornia.org

CONTENTS

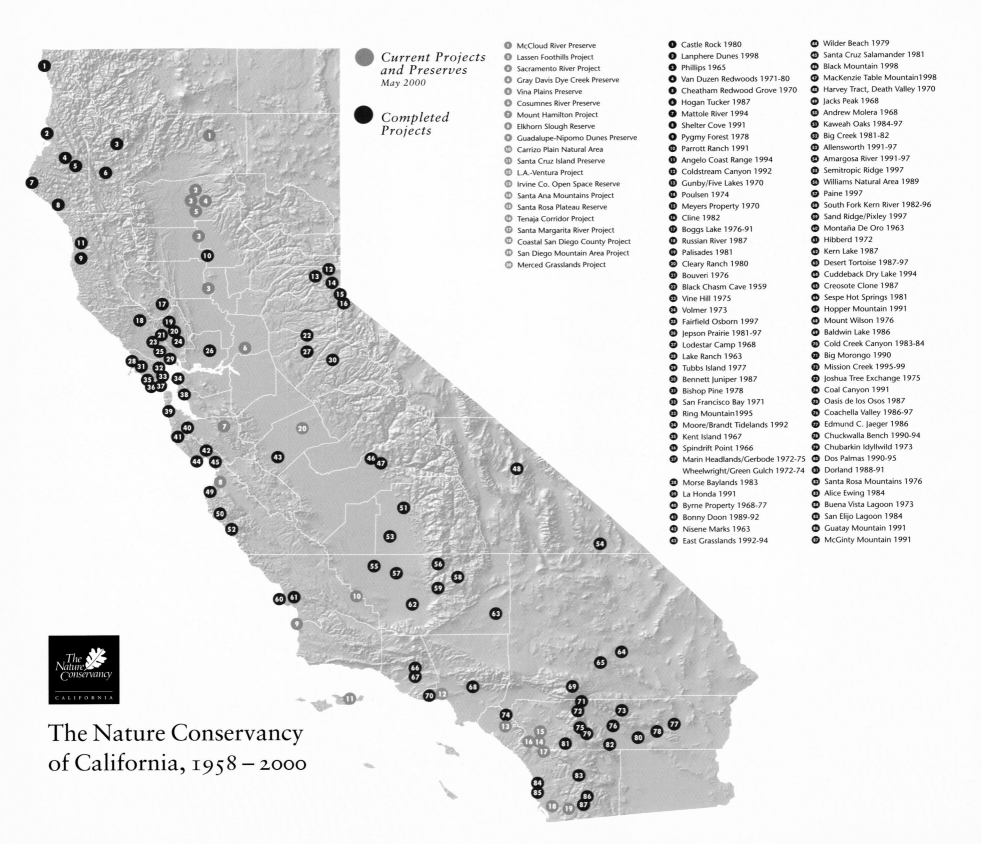

Current Projects and Preserves
May 2000

Completed Projects

1. McCloud River Preserve
2. Lassen Foothills Project
3. Sacramento River Project
4. Gray Davis Dye Creek Preserve
5. Vina Plains Preserve
6. Cosumnes River Preserve
7. Mount Hamilton Project
8. Elkhorn Slough Reserve
9. Guadalupe-Nipomo Dunes Preserve
10. Carrizo Plain Natural Area
11. Santa Cruz Island Preserve
12. L.A.-Ventura Project
13. Irvine Co. Open Space Reserve
14. Santa Ana Mountains Project
15. Santa Rosa Plateau Reserve
16. Tenaja Corridor Project
17. Santa Margarita River Project
18. Coastal San Diego County Project
19. San Diego Mountain Area Project
20. Merced Grasslands Project

1. Castle Rock 1980
2. Lanphere Dunes 1998
3. Phillips 1965
4. Van Duzen Redwoods 1971-80
5. Cheatham Redwood Grove 1970
6. Hogan Tucker 1987
7. Mattole River 1994
8. Shelter Cove 1991
9. Pygmy Forest 1978
10. Parrott Ranch 1991
11. Angelo Coast Range 1994
12. Coldstream Canyon 1992
13. Gunby/Five Lakes 1970
14. Poulsen 1974
15. Meyers Property 1970
16. Cline 1982
17. Boggs Lake 1976-91
18. Russian River 1987
19. Palisades 1981
20. Cleary Ranch 1980
21. Bouveri 1976
22. Black Chasm Cave 1959
23. Vine Hill 1975
24. Volmer 1973
25. Fairfield Osborn 1997
26. Jepson Prairie 1981-97
27. Lodestar Camp 1968
28. Lake Ranch 1963
29. Tubbs Island 1977
30. Bennett Juniper 1987
31. Bishop Pine 1978
32. San Francisco Bay 1971
33. Ring Mountain 1995
34. Moore/Brandt Tidelands 1992
35. Kent Island 1967
36. Spindrift Point 1966
37. Marin Headlands/Gerbode 1972-75
   Wheelwright/Green Gulch 1972-74
38. Morse Baylands 1983
39. La Honda 1991
40. Byrne Property 1968-77
41. Bonny Doon 1989-92
42. Nisene Marks 1963
43. East Grasslands 1992-94

44. Wilder Beach 1979
45. Santa Cruz Salamander 1981
46. Black Mountain 1998
47. MacKenzie Table Mountain 1998
48. Harvey Tract, Death Valley 1970
49. Jacks Peak 1968
50. Andrew Molera 1968
51. Kaweah Oaks 1984-97
52. Big Creek 1981-82
53. Allensworth 1991-97
54. Amargosa River 1991-97
55. Semitropic Ridge 1997
56. Williams Natural Area 1989
57. Paine 1997
58. South Fork Kern River 1982-96
59. Sand Ridge/Pixley 1997
60. Montaña De Oro 1963
61. Hibberd 1972
62. Kern Lake 1987
63. Desert Tortoise 1987-97
64. Cuddeback Dry Lake 1994
65. Creosote Clone 1987
66. Sespe Hot Springs 1981
67. Hopper Mountain 1991
68. Mount Wilson 1976
69. Baldwin Lake 1986
70. Cold Creek Canyon 1983-84
71. Big Morongo 1990
72. Mission Creek 1995-99
73. Joshua Tree Exchange 1975
74. Coal Canyon 1991
75. Oasis de los Osos 1987
76. Coachella Valley 1986-97
77. Edmund C. Jaeger 1986
78. Chuckwalla Bench 1990-94
79. Chubarkin Idyllwild 1973
80. Dos Palmas 1990-95
81. Dorland 1988-91
82. Santa Rosa Mountains 1976
83. Alice Ewing 1984
84. Buena Vista Lagoon 1973
85. San Elijo Lagoon 1984
86. Guatay Mountain 1991
87. McGinty Mountain 1991

The Nature Conservancy
of California, 1958 – 2000

INTRODUCTION

California…a Land Apart

ONE WAY TO UNDERSTAND THE SCOPE AND GRANDEUR OF THIS STATE'S lands and waters is to think of California as its own world, isolated on the edge of the continent by alpine peaks and shimmering deserts. Within its borders are vast grasslands, rugged foothills, lush forests, oak woodlands, teeming marshes and sloughs, billowing dunes. California's natural landscapes are so rich and diverse that they harbor more native species of plants and animals—and more native species at risk—than any other state.

Yes, many of California's unique lands, rivers, streams, coastal waters, and the native species they support are at risk of being lost forever. The clock is ticking. Imagine all the present inhabitants of New York State deciding to settle in California. Growth of that magnitude is forecast; our population is expected to mushroom from 32 million to 50 million people by the year 2025.

Safeguarding California's landscapes and native species is essential—right now, before it's too late. That is the mission of our California chapter of The Nature Conservancy, a private, non-profit organization and one of the world's leading conservation groups.

We believe that growth does not need to overwhelm California's natural areas. We also believe that a robust economy and healthy natural landscapes must go hand in hand in the twenty-first century. We invite farmers, ranchers, and business people to be our partners. They, along with public agencies, local conservation organizations, universities, foundations, and individual donors, join with us to achieve mutual conservation goals. Basing our work on sound science and careful planning, we use nonconfrontational, market-based economic solutions to protect the best examples of every vital natural community represented in the state.

The effort to save our wildlands, open spaces, and native species is being made on multiple fronts. One of them is this book, *Native Grandeur.* In it we celebrate California's natural wonders and survey conservation successes and challenges, but the book's message includes a call to action. The evocative nineteenth- and early twentieth-century landscape paintings that illustrate this volume enhance our appreciation of California's natural beauty, deepen our concern about the fate of its marvelous landscapes, and strengthen our determination to safeguard them for future generations.

The Nature Conservancy of California is proud to present *Native Grandeur*. We are deeply indebted to Joan Irvine Smith, whose thoughts inspired this work and who furnished from her own collection and from that of The Irvine Museum most of the beautiful paintings that grace its pages. We are grateful as well to the other museums, galleries, and private collectors that granted us permission to reproduce paintings from their collections. Finally, we are especially grateful to the Joan Irvine Smith and Athalie R. Clarke Foundation for underwriting the cost of preparing and printing the book.

This handsome volume, with its resplendent paintings, reminds us how important it is to preserve California's landscapes as more than just framed memories. In it we find inspiration and a renewed sense of purpose. Much important work remains to be done.

DONN B. MILLER
Chairman of the Board
The Nature Conservancy of California

FOREWORD

California's Living Landscapes

BY EDWARD O. WILSON

LIKE FEW OTHER PLACES IN THE WORLD, THE NATURAL LANDSCAPES of California invite celebration by the visual arts. In topographic and climatic diversity, the state resembles a small continent: edged by the Pacific on its western border, high mountains to the east, and the Mojave Desert to the south. Each latitudinal transect taken at 200-mile intervals from the Klamath Mountains south to San Diego traces a separate journey of exceptional beauty.

It has been said that the human species evolved to live where citruses grow. California is one of only five regions of the world with a Mediterranean climate, sharing that blessing with central Chile, the Western Cape of South Africa, southwestern and south-central Australia, and the Mediterranean basin itself. Each has a rich assemblage of animal species, but the flora is in each case the crown jewel. Africa south of the Cunene and Zambesi Rivers, for example, has about 30,000 species of flowering plants, 60 percent endemic to the region, to which the Western Cape is a disproportionate contributor. California, or more precisely the California Floristic Province stretching from southern Oregon to Baja California, has a comparable distinction in relation to the rest of North America. Its approximately 4,300 species of flowering plants make up one-fourth of all those occurring in the United States and Canada combined, and half are endemic to the California Province — in other words, found nowhere else. Its major vegetation types, including redwood forest, coastal scrub, oak woodland, chaparral, and desert, differ strikingly in appearance and species composition one from the other.

Californians have awakened, unfortunately too late for a few of the living landscapes, to the extraordinary value of their ancient wild heritage. Scientists who study biological diversity offer strong practical reasons for conserving all of it, including especially the economic and medical potential in products from wild species, and the free but vital services natural ecosystems provide in building soil, cleansing water, and, indeed, generating the very air we breathe. But they all also agree that the aesthetic and spiritual value wildlands provide, and California possesses in fortunate abundance, are equally important to human welfare. To capture and give immediacy to this important part of our lives is one of the great and unique roles of the visual arts. To depict biodiversity as it most powerfully strikes the eye is to unite science and the humanities in a common purpose.

PREFACE

Reflections on the Irvine Ranch

BY JOAN IRVINE SMITH

MY GREAT-GRANDFATHER, JAMES IRVINE I, WAS BORN IN BELFAST, IRELAND, in 1827, of Scotch-Irish Presbyterian descent. His father was a man of modest income, and he was next to the youngest in a family of nine children. In 1846, he immigrated to the United States and worked for two years in a paper mill in New York until he caught Gold Fever and joined the stampede to California in 1849. He elected to go by way of the Isthmus of Panama and caught passage north to San Francisco on a clipper ship. Among his companions were Collis P. Huntington and Dr. Benjamin Flint. The latter association eventually led to the creation of the Irvine Ranch.

In 1848, at the end of the Mexican-American War, California had become an American possession and gradually the large ranchos were broken up and sold to Americans who were coming to California in steadily growing numbers. When California became a state two years later, westward migration increased rapidly on the promise of possible riches and available new lands. Although most of this boom occurred in northern California as a result of the Gold Rush, a little agricultural pueblo on the Los Angeles River also grew and was incorporated as the City of Los Angeles in 1850.

Growth slowed in the 1860s. Westward migration declined as a result of the Civil War and renewed Indian attacks, and surveys of possible railroad routes to California were suspended. Severe flooding inundated the Coastal Plain in 1861, and only a few years later, many of the large ranchero holdings were devastated by the Great Drought of 1863-64. The Arcadian Era in southern California had come to an end.

For a time, my great-grandfather, James I, worked as both miner and merchant in the gold fields. He later moved to San Francisco where he became a successful produce merchant and invested well in San Francisco real estate. In 1864, he joined with Llewellyn Bixby and Benjamin and Thomas Flint, who had become prosperous as sheep men, to purchase the three Spanish land grants: the Rancho San Joaquin, the Rancho Lomas de Santiago, and a portion of the Rancho Santiago de Santa Ana. Covering roughly 115,000 acres and reaching from the ocean to the San Bernardino County line, twenty miles long and nine and a half miles wide, these three tracts of land were eventu-

Raymond Nott (1888-1948)
Laguna Coast
oil on canvas, 48 x 60 inches
Joan Irvine Smith Collection

William Wendt (1865-1946)
Santa Ana River
oil on canvas, 25 x 30 inches
Private collection, courtesy of
The Irvine Museum

ally to become the Irvine Ranch, comprising one-fifth of what is today Orange County.

In the early 1800s, Spain had begun to encourage private development of land in southern California by issuing land grants. During the remainder of the Spanish Regime, ending in 1821, and for the first ten or twelve years of Mexican rule, about thirty private rancho grants were made in all of California. The first Spanish land grant in what is now Orange County was the Rancho Santiago de Santa Ana, given to Jose Antonio Yorba and Juan Pablo Peralta in 1810. This rancho included the lands around the confluence of the Santa Ana River and Santiago Creek, an area that now encompasses the City of Santa Ana.

In 1833, the missions were secularized and their vast holdings were either returned to the public domain or incorporated into existing ranchos. At that time, much of the land in the Santa Ana and San Gabriel River watersheds was covered by herds of cattle grazing on large ranchos. In 1846, the last Mexican governor of Alta California, Pio Pico, issued a private grant to Theodosio Yorba for the adjoining Rancho Lomas de Santiago. Falling within the grant was the magnificent grove of ancient coastal oaks still standing in present-day Irvine Park.

A variety of wild visitors then roamed the area and were accustomed to watering at the springs in the future park. Interestingly, both brown bears and grizzlies enjoyed a plentiful supply of grapes, berries, and acorns in the grove. Normally mortal enemies, both bears' presence in the same habitat is biologically unique to the Santa Ana Mountains.

Occasionally, a grizzly would bring down a young steer for a change of diet. In such instances, the rancher would call upon Jose Sepúlveda, owner of the neighboring Rancho San Joaquin, whose hard-riding vaqueros were keen on roping rogue bears. A favorite spot for this daring sport was the valley in Santiago Canyon that forms present-day Irvine Lake. Cougars frequently mauled stock, and coyote packs ran down and hamstrung calves. Most destructive and elusive of all was a pack of timber wolves in Peters Canyon, which was finally eliminated by poison.

By the same token, the hills and valleys were a hunter's paradise. Deer, dove, quail, ducks, and geese abounded, and even a few antelope could be found in the canyons and on the nearby plains. Today, a pair of cougars, and Samson, a black bear captured in a swimming pool in Monrovia, reside in the park zoo and recapture a portion

Edgar Payne (1883-1947)
Sycamore in Autumn, Orange County Park
oil on board, 32 x 42 inches
Private collection, courtesy of The Irvine Museum

of Orange County's vanishing wildlife and the park's first "picnickers."

Because of the disruption of the cotton industry in the South caused by the Civil War, wool was in great demand. Consequently, my great-grandfather and his three partners brought in thousands of head of sheep and imported twenty-five Spanish Merino bucks and ewes from the Sandwich Islands, now known as the Hawaiian Islands, to stock their newly acquired ranchos. Soon, the bleating of lambs replaced the bawling of calves as sheep took the place of longhorns on the hills and around the water holes beneath the oaks.

Shortly after it became a sheep camp, the future park in Santiago Canyon was "discovered" by the first settlers in the Santa Ana Valley. The German burghers of

Emil Kosa, Jr. (1903-1968)
The Sun Was Everywhere
oil on canvas, 27-1/4 x 38-1/4 inches
Joan Irvine Smith Collection

Anaheim, who had planted grapes and established a wine colony in 1857, were the earliest to stake a recreational claim on the site. They called the place "the Picnic Grounds," a name that would stick for the next quarter-century.

By 1876, my great-grandfather bought out his three partners' one-half interest in the holdings for $150,000. That same year marked two literary tributes to the future Irvine Park. Curiously, the first was published in the *Gazeta Polska*, in Warsaw. The author's name was Henryk Sienkiewicz, later to win immortality and a Nobel Prize for his epic of Rome *Quo Vadis*. While visiting a short-lived artists' colony of Poles in Anaheim, Sienkiewicz was drawn to the Santiago by reports of its *ursus horribilis* (grizzly bear). Of what is now Irvine Park he wrote,

> "This valley embracing about two square miles, was not so overgrown with dense entangled vegetation as the others. It was, in fact a Versailles garden in the wilderness, embellished with marvelous bouquets of trees and shrubs, almost as through contrived by the hand of a gardener artist."

Equally lyrical was a passage written by the distinguished Polish Shakespearean actress Madame Helena Modjeska, a dozen years before she bought the canyon that bears her name. In 1876, she described the "Picnic Grounds" as "a charming spot of green meadows with clean, limpid brooks."

By the mid 1880s, the semi-frontier conditions were rapidly giving way in the Santa Ana Valley, as elsewhere in southern California, to a more advanced social and economic order. The completion of the Southern Pacific Railroad to Los Angeles in 1876, and the coming of the Santa Fe Railway nine years later, changed the agricultural outlook for the Los Angeles-Santa Ana Basin, brought about a large influx of population, stimulated the subdivision of many large land holdings, and ushered in the great boom of 1886-88.

But my great-grandfather, founder of the Irvine Ranch, was not permitted to participate to any degree in these new developments, as he died in San Francisco on March 15, 1886. Under the provisions of his father's will, my grandfather, James Irvine II, who was then 18 years of age, had seven long years to wait to claim his inheritance.

In 1887, the Trustees of the estate put the Irvine Ranch up for public auction. On April 16, 1887, the Trustees "offered and agreed to sell" at least 100,000 acres of the Irvine Ranch in Los Angeles County at public auction. The bidding began at $1,300,000 and had reached $1,385,000 when the timekeeper became confused as to which of the two bidders

William Wendt (1865-1946)
Laguna Hills, 1928
oil on canvas, 25 x 30 inches
Private collection, courtesy of The Irvine Museum

had made the final bid. When the decision was challenged in court, the judge ruled that neither bidder was entitled to the land. Though the Trustees refused either offer, they soon renewed their efforts to sell the property, either as a whole or in separate parcels.

Under the Irvine-Flint-Bixby Partnership, the property had been used almost entirely for the pasturage of sheep, but by 1878 a small amount of the land had begun to be devoted to tenant farming. Although sheep raising continued as an important business long after the death of James I, the large flocks of earlier years had dwindled and been replaced by a substantial number of cattle. Much of the range land was leased to outsiders and the Irvine Ranch was fast undergoing a radical transition from a grazing and pastoral stage to a farming economy that characterized the general agricultural development of most of southern California.

As the decade ended, in 1886 and 1888, a withering blight affected both the valley and the "Picnic Grounds," ending commercial grape growing and ushering in citrus. Even the wild grapes in the canyons disappeared. With them went part of the primeval charm of the "Picnic Grounds," for vines once choked nearly every tree. Today, a tiny sample of this jungle-like setting is preserved by the vines that garland the oaks northwest of the boat lake.

In 1889, the citizens of the Santa Ana Valley, after several attempts, broke off from Los Angeles County and created the County of Orange. That year, "the heavens broke loose" as the *Santa Ana Weekly Blade* exclaimed, and long-continued rains caused serious floods in many parts of southern California. The Los Angeles, San Gabriel, and Santa Ana Rivers went on a wild rampage. Bridges, railroad tracks, houses, and farmlands were washed away.

The Trustees continued their efforts to sell the ranch, but negotiations dragged on and time ran out. In 1893, my grandfather James Irvine II, came into full possession of the property and was to retain complete control and direction over the ranch until his death well over a half a century later. On June 4, 1894, he incorporated his holdings as the Irvine Company under the laws of the state of West Virginia. Astute, but shy, my grandfather, who within 15 years diversified his father's pastures into the most productive agricultural empire in the state, always described himself as "just a farmer."

Reflecting his Scottish heritage, my grandfather's frugality was legendary. Less well-known was his great love of nature, a sentiment uncommon to most of his contemporaries. If an oak tree intruded upon a projected road widening, he would reroute the road rather than remove the tree. Not surprisingly, the "Picnic Grounds" became the pride of his great ranch. It was the personal retreat of both my grandfather and my grandmother Anita Plum, and the private playground of their two eldest children, my father James Irvine Jr., known as "Jase," and my aunt Katherine. Their youngest child, my uncle Myford, was not born until 1898.

William A. Griffith
(1866-1940)
The Bean Ranch
oil on canvas,
30-1/2 x
40-1/4 inches
The Irvine
Museum

Knowing my grandfather's fondness for the site, charges that he was selfish pale in the light of what became known as "The Gift Munificent." In April 1897, he gave Orange County 160 acres in Santiago Canyon, containing the "Picnic Grounds," for a public park. The new park, now called Irvine Regional Park and totaling 477 acres, was the first county park in California, and became the envy of the state.

The gift came with only a few conditions: a road which had bisected the grove was to be relocated on the north side, thus becoming the park's first entrance; the grounds were to be fenced and an "inspector" to be appointed, to keep out sheepherders and woodchoppers; no intoxicating liquors were to be sold on the premises; admission was to be free; and, above all, my grandfather stipulated that the trees should receive good care and that the grounds should be kept as natural as possible.

Dogs are still welcome in the park, and this would certainly please my grandfather, as he was particularly fond of them. An avid bird shooter, he kept over a dozen Irish setters and English pointers for hunting the vast number of quail and dove that populated the ranch and the swarms of ducks and geese that migrated through the property each fall on their way south. My grandfather even kept a large aviary behind the ranch house in Tustin, where injured game birds were kept until they had recovered and could be released into the wild.

On October 3, 1997, the 100th anniversary of the park, a commemorative statue of James Irvine II was unveiled to a gathering of Irvine family members, invited dignitaries, and guests. The monumental bronze, by noted sculptor Deborah C. Fellows, was commissioned by the family and depicts my grandfather in a typical hunting pose, shotgun in hand, flanked by his ever-present dogs. Titled "The Winds of Change," the figure reflects

Deborah C. Fellows, sculptor
The Winds of Change, 1997
Monumental bronze statue of
James Irvine at Irvine Park

on the park's progress in the course of a century and will forever stand as its guardian protector.

When my grandfather died, on August 24, 1947, my uncle Myford Irvine succeeded him as president of the Irvine Company. By the time I joined the Irvine Company Board of Directors in 1957, the blight of urban sprawl had already begun to overrun Los Angeles County.

As development of the Irvine Ranch was not only timely but inevitable, I urged my fellow directors to adopt a Master Plan for the property in order to avoid the mistakes that had occurred in Los Angeles and other areas. The plan I envisioned would combine residential, commercial, and industrial development with greenbelts, parks, and large, natural open-space areas that would preserve the beauty of the land and also the native plants and animals that existed there. In other words, a plan that would balance economic growth and environmental preservation.

When Myford Irvine died on January 11, 1959, the James Irvine Foundation gained absolute domination and control over the Irvine Company. Nevertheless, in December of 1959, I won a two-year battle to convince my fellow directors to make a gift of 1,000 acres of land to the University of California for a new campus on the Irvine Ranch, and in December of 1960, won a three-year battle for a master development plan for the Irvine Ranch lands. The Irvine Company retained the firm of William L. Pereira and Associates, architects for the new university campus at Irvine, to prepare a Master Plan for the entire ranch.

Today, conserving the environment and preserving the imperiled diversity of life on our planet are two of the most important issues facing humankind. The need to balance economic growth with environmental preservation has become our most pressing obligation. To achieve a balance between nature and humankind, the environmental community must recognize the necessity of a strong and

Guy Rose (1867-1925)
Laguna Eucalyptus, c.1917
oil on canvas, 40 x 30 inches
The Irvine Museum

productive economy that will support environmental projects, and the development community must serve its own enlightened self-interest by pursuing a positive environmental approach. Only by doing our part to preserve California's vanishing natural landscape can we be sure that our grandchildren will experience these wild places first-hand, and not merely through paintings like those in this book.

The glorification of nature is a universal theme in the history of art. In the United States, landscape painting is a time-honored tradition inseparable from the spirit of American art. In the early 1800s, at the time of the Industrial Revolution, a group of dedicated landscape painters, called the Hudson River School, ventured into what was then the wilderness of the Hudson River Valley. Lamenting the destruction of the natural environment, they painted scenes of virgin and unspoiled countryside. In their own way, they were the first environmental activists.

In California, a similar group of spiritually aware painters recorded the beauty of nature in the early 1900s. One of the most prominent of these artists, William Wendt (1865-1946) believed that nature was a manifestation of God and viewed himself as nature's faithful interpreter.

But by the 1930s, art no longer paid homage to nature. The artists turned to the cities and the material attributes of the modern age for inspiration. It is said that art mirrors society. When we supplanted our regard for nature with more material concerns, we placed out trust in technology and undervalued the importance of the natural environment. Today, with the renaissance of the glorification of nature in art, that spirit is motivating enlightened people in the same way it energized artists nearly a hundred years ago. The common bond is a deep reverence for nature, and the common goal is to preserve our environment. No statement is more eloquent than the silent testament of these magnificent paintings. Each generation, in its turn, is the steward of the land, water, and air. Our time is now.

William Wendt (1865-1946)
Along the River Bed
oil on canvas, 30 x 40 inches
Joan Irvine Smith Collection

THE SOUTH COAST

A New Approach to Conservation

IN 1913, AN ENGLISH IMMIGRANT, J. SMEATON CHASE, TOOK a horseback journey along the coast of southern California. When he reached the San Fernando Valley, Chase recounted that it stretched away "in league upon league of grain."

Today, if you retrace Chase's hoofprints, you will not be tromping through wheat or rye. The San Fernando Valley—the demographic center of California—is often considered America's prototypical suburb. Here, only asphalt and brake lights stretch for league upon league. Far from reveling in the freedom of Chase's open trail, you more likely will feel awash in a sea of humanity. Indeed, with the population of southern California at 20 million and rising, elbow room anywhere along the South Coast has become a precious commodity.

But lift your eyes, and you might also see a green horizon. Mountains ring the San Fernando Valley. These hills are not some painted backdrop, the product of a Hollywood dream factory. They are the genuine item, replete with nearly impenetrable thickets of scrub oak, sage, and chamise. Overhead, hawks keen. The underbrush rustles with quail, roadrunners, ground squirrels, rattlesnakes. Although housing has carved up many slopes, some hills retain their natural state, and they may remain forever unscathed—for here in southern California, the land where real estate reigns supreme and the bulldozer is top predator, momentum is gathering to save open space.

The South Coast is a land of dramatic topography. A cluster of mountain ranges, all bearing names that echo California's Spanish heritage, combines with the Mojave and Sonoran Deserts to isolate the South Coast from the rest of California. These steep young mountains, most less than a million years old—pipsqueaks in geologic time—ring large, flat alluvial valleys.

Paul Grimm (1892-1974)
Beverly Hills
oil on canvas, 25 x 30 inches
Private collection courtesy of
The Irvine Museum

WHEN THE SUNLIGHT is not screened and filtered by the moisture-laden air, the land is revealed in all its semi-arid poverty. The bald sculptured mountains stand forth in a harsh and glaring light. But let the light turn soft with ocean mist, and miraculous changes occur. The bare mountain ranges, appallingly harsh in contour, suddenly become wrapped in an entrancing ever-changing loveliness of light and shadow; the most commonplace objects assume a matchless perfection of form; and the land itself becomes a thing of beauty. The color of the land is in the light and the light is somehow artificial and controlled. Things are not killed by the sunlight, as in a desert; they merely dry up. A desert light brings out the sharpness of point, angles, and forms. But this is not a desert light nor is it a tropical for it has neutral tones. It is Southern California light and it has no counterpart in the world.

— **CAREY MCWILLIAMS,**
Southern California:
An Island on the Land
(Salt Lake City: Gibbs Smith,
Publisher [Peregrine Smith
Books], 1983.)
Used with permission.

Frank Cuprien (1871-1948)
Golden Sunset, near
Portuguese Bend
oil on canvas, 30 x 40 inches
Courtesy of DeRu's Fine Arts,
Laguna Beach

Deep canyons score the mountainsides, eroded by the kind of seasonal stream that prompted Mark Twain to declare he had fallen into a California river and "come out all dusty." Twain probably stumbled in the summer, for when winter storms blow in from the Pacific, southern California's sleepy creeks and washes can erupt into raging cataracts, sending boulders the size of cars—and sometimes even cars themselves—caroming downstream. In 1943 the San Gabriel Mountains received twenty-six inches of rain in a single day, a world record that stood for decades.

Usually, the South Coast is not so damp. Typically, the sun shines 350 days a year. Summer temperatures regularly break 100 degrees, while winter frosts are rare. Sun worshippers and beachgoers call this set of weather conditions nirvana. Climatologists call it Mediterranean.

Only five similar regions exist in the world, and they all support a rich collection of plant and animal life adapted to extremes of heat as well as to the wildfires that periodically char the landscape. California's Mediterranean climate zone, which spans most of the state, is home to more than 76,000 plant species. Of these, 2,000 grow nowhere else in the world. San Diego County alone is home to more species of plants and animals than any other county in the United States.

For more than twenty years, The Nature Conservancy has been working to preserve the South Coast's precious natural heritage. In 1978, the Conservancy protected ninety percent of Santa Cruz Island, the largest of southern California's Channel Islands, sometimes called the "American Galapagos" because of the rich diversity of their wildlife. Recently the U.S. National Park Service acquired the remaining ten percent of the island.

Eleven species of plants and animals are unique to Santa Cruz Island, and the island supports seventy other species found only on the Channel Islands. Decades of sheep grazing and a proliferation of exotic plants have degraded the island's vegetation, but The Nature Conservancy has removed the sheep and is restoring the island's fragile ecosystem with a program that emphasizes controlled burns. With the sheep gone, new forests of Bishop pine are spreading across what were once bare, eroded hillsides. The Santa Cruz Island silver lotus, a plant that until recently grew nowhere in the world except on a few Santa Cruz Island cliff faces, has dramatically expanded its range.

One of the most unusual residents of the island is the Santa Cruz Island fox. About the size of a housecat, the island fox is threatened with extinction by the presence of wild pigs and golden eagles. In the mid-1800s, pigs were introduced to Santa Cruz Island and later allowed to run wild. Traditionally, bald eagles have also lived on Santa Cruz Island. Although they are marine feeders with no interest in pigs or foxes, the bald eagles prevented golden eagles from invading their territory. Unfortunately, the island's bald eagles succumbed to DDT, and recently golden eagles have colonized the island. Attracted by the presence of feral pigs, golden eagles also prey on the island fox, an easy target because it hunts by day. In cooperation with the National Park Service, the Conservancy is now attempting the complex task of restoring the ecological status quo by relocating the golden eagles and removing the feral pigs.

Guy Rose (1867-1925)
Indian Tobacco Trees, La Jolla
oil on canvas, 24 x 29 inches
Joan Irvine Smith Collection

In 1984 The Nature Conservancy established the Santa Rosa Plateau Ecological Reserve in western Riverside County. Here amid flat mesas and rolling hills, Engelmann oaks abound. Often cited as the most endangered tree in California, this craggy oak flourished from Oregon to Baja in prehistoric times. Even in the early twentieth century, Engelmann oaks were still widespread throughout southern California. Once common near Pasadena, the Engelmann oak's distinctive, angular limbs came to symbolize the Arts and Crafts movement, centered in that city. Unfortunately, development has all but obliterated the Engelmann oak from its historic range, including Pasadena. Only two significant stands survive, one in San Diego County, where The Nature Conservancy is also active, and the other on the Santa Rosa Plateau.

Elmer Wachtel (1864-1929)
Golden Autumn, Cajon Pass
oil on canvas, 22 x 30 inches
Private collection,
courtesy of The Irvine Museum

In recent years, scientists have come to understand that isolated wild lands cannot survive forever. Harvard biologist Edward O. Wilson pioneered this field of research after studying plant and animal populations on Pacific islands. He theorized that the smaller an island and the more distant it is from land, the fewer species it can support. Soon he and other scientists applied these findings to any island of land, whether it is surrounded by the Pacific Ocean or a sea of red-tiled roofs. The dangers proved to be the same. Genetic inbreeding weakens the island's plant and animal populations, and catastrophic events such as storms, fires, or disease can reduce a weakened species to the point where its numbers never rebound. The solution—at least for islands on the land—is to establish corridors of wild country linking protected regions, so species can migrate and gain access to a wider gene pool.

Guided by this concept, The Nature Conservancy has been thinking big in the vicinity of the Santa Rosa Plateau. Here the Conservancy hopes to secure entire landscapes and connect them with wildlife corridors. On the Santa Rosa Plateau, many streams drain into the Santa Margarita River. The Conservancy has partnered with neighboring Camp Pendleton Marine Base and several other organizations to protect lands along the main stem of the Santa Margarita, which passes through a steep mountain canyon lined with cottonwoods, alder, and sycamore. In 1998, after purchasing the last major privately owned parcel along the Santa Margarita, The Nature Conservancy conveyed the property to San Diego State University, so it could be included in a large ecological preserve the university manages. The Nature Conservancy often functions as this kind of intermediary, acquiring a property and then transferring it to another organization with similar goals.

To the west of the Santa Rosa Plateau lies a large section of Cleveland National Forest. Mountain lions, bobcats, mule deer, badgers, and many smaller animals migrate between these regions along a three-mile strip of land called the "Tenaja Corridor." Tenajas—deep tanks scoured into creek beds—are a distinctive feature of the Santa Rosa countryside. In summer months, long after a creek has grown quiet and dusty, tenajas hold water. These small reservoirs are crucial to the survival of creatures like the southwestern pond turtle and the endangered red-legged frog.

Residential construction, commercial development, and road building besiege the Tenaja Corridor. In a novel approach to land conservation, the Conservancy has bought critical properties in the corridor before they could be developed, carved residential lots from this acreage, and then sought out buyers for these plots. But only the conservation-minded need apply. In return for a secluded country home, owners must accept what are called conservation easements: permanent restrictions placed on deeds to protect the land from future development. Easements on the Tenaja Corridor are specifically designed to promote the free flow of wildlife. Subdivision and fencing are limited, and the introduction of invasive plants forbidden. With any luck these legal encumbrances will make good neighbors of men and mountain lions, though the big cats are not required to sign any binding agreements.

Heading west from the Santa Rosa Plateau, you descend into rolling hills characterized by a distinct ecosystem known as coastal sage scrub. Once this shrubby mix of cactus, buckwheat, and coastal sagebrush covered millions of acres of California's coastal hills. Now that range has been reduced to several hundred thousand acres, much of it degraded. Though it seems nondescript to a casual observer, coastal sage scrub supports many unique species, most

William Wendt (1865-1946)
Ranch in the Valley, c. 1928
oil on canvas, 30 x 40 inches
Private collection, courtesy of
The Irvine Museum

notably a songbird no more than four inches long called the California gnatcatcher.

Along the coastal hills of Orange County, some large tracts of coastal sage scrub have survived intact. In the early 1990s, when real estate development threatened these last open spaces, environmentalists petitioned the federal government to declare the California gnatcatcher endangered.

Hoping to prevent the bitter antagonism that has characterized endangered species conflicts elsewhere in the United States, The Nature Conservancy decided to participate in Natural Community Conservation Planning (NCCP), an experimental state program designed to resolve environmental disputes by allowing all interested parties to plan for both development and conservation. Operating with funding from several foundations, the Conservancy and its partner organizations in Orange County helped bring together builders and environmentalists—often implacable opponents—along with local, state, and federal agencies. What emerged from this dialogue was a revolutionary approach to preserving natural communities.

Basing land-use decisions on the viability of ecosystems, an NCCP planning group worked with the Irvine Company, the major private landholder in the region, to develop and manage a system of large, interconnected coastal sage scrub reserves stretching from the oak woodlands of the Santa Ana Mountains to the scrubby bluffs of Laguna Beach. To implement this plan, local jurisdictions in Orange County set aside 17,000 acres, mostly in the form of county and state parks. The Irvine Company contributed 21,000 acres. In return it received something equally precious—a stable legal footing. The land the Irvine Company still owns will not be subject to any future demands for wildlife protection unless the public is willing to pick up the tab.

Describing the NCCP process, Monica Florian, vice president of Corporate Affairs for the Irvine Company, said, "The Nature Conservancy was invaluable, not only because of their conservation expertise but also their ability to bring us all to consensus, to keep people at the table through all the hard parts." The Conservancy's Steve Johnson summed up the Orange County negotiations, declaring, "NCCP shows you can bring all the parties together and work out a practical, no-nonsense plan that puts endangered species conflict to rest."

Currently, The Nature Conservancy administers the Irvine Company

Paul Lauritz (1889-1975)
Autumn near Big Bear Lake
oil on canvas, 28 x 34 inches
The Irvine Museum

Open Space Reserve, the first time the Conservancy has partnered with a corporation to protect an endangered California landscape. Here on the rolling coastal hills, California gnatcatchers continue their lives undisturbed while hikers stroll tawny grasslands or wander through woodlands to a chorus of towhees, scrub jays, wrens, thrushes, vireos, nuthatches, and woodpeckers.

U. S. Secretary of the Interior Bruce Babbitt called the Irvine Company Open Space Reserve "a real triumph of communities over conflict." Not surprisingly, the NCCP approach to habitat conservation has

William Wendt (1865-1946)
Crystal Cove
oil on canvas, 28 x 36 inches
Private collection,
courtesy of The Irvine Museum

caught on throughout southern California. Riverside and San Bernardino counties are developing habitat plans. Los Angeles is crafting a small plan for Palos Verdes Peninsula. Orange County has turned its attention to another large stretch of land near Camp Pendleton. The biggest NCCP of all, however, is San Diego's Multiple Species Conservation Program (MSCP).

The scale and complexity of the San Diego plan distinguishes it from Orange County's. The land in question is approximately 900

Frederick Melville Dumond
(1867-1927)
Laguna Beach, 1911
oil on canvas, 24 x 36 inches
The Irvine Museum

Voice from the Urban Wilderness

LOS ANGELES WOULD BE PARADISE with about 9 million fewer people. The snow-capped peaks within view of our homes, our workplaces, and our beaches can't be seen through the haze most of the year. Our rivers are trapezoidal concrete channels, rich in trash and poor in fish. Crows, and perhaps rats, are the most abundant wildlife seen near our house.

This is one of the most diverse cities in the world in terms of human population, and one of the most diverse areas of the United States in terms of wildlife. Mountain peaks over 10,000 feet high are within miles of an ocean edge that drops off sharply into the deep Pacific; the variety of landscapes creates a magnificent range of habitats. Our active geology, thanks to the San Andreas fault, keeps our landscape moving; the convergence of three weather patterns creates dynamic climate zones; and our position on the Pacific Rim has made Los Angeles a Mecca for people from all over the world. It's said that what happens culturally, economically, and socially in Los Angeles rolls across the country like a wave. Will we, as a diverse population, be able to lead the way in saving our wildlife and landscapes?

Elmer Wachtel (1864-1929)
Azusa Wash, c. 1910
oil on canvas, 20 x 30 inches
The Irvine Museum

We want to see steelhead trout running the Los Angeles River again. The stark beauty of our brown hills and canyons, and the slumping cliffs along our coast, can yet be protected. We can rein in our sprawl and save a few more oak trees. Sea otters can return to our coastal waters. Our groundwater can be pure and safe. I believe that we can do it.

If each of us takes on one issue, large or small, that we care about passionately, what could happen? Be it better public transportation, protecting a coastline, or restoring the neighborhood creek, if we each hang on tenaciously to that one cause—after five years, after ten years, think how far we could get.

—HEATHER TRIM, *geologist and mom*

square miles, three times the size of the Irvine Company project. The Orange County negotiations focused on a single private entity, while the MSCP could potentially affect 20,000 private landowners. The ecological issues are equally daunting. Because of the extraordinary diversity of San Diego's natural communities, biologists developing the MSCP must weigh the fate of at least 100 different species.

After years of discussion, a welter of interested individuals and organizations hammered together a plan that protects 172,000 acres spanning five separate political jurisdictions. That acreage should increase substantially when the MSCP is joined to four other NCCP projects now planned or proposed for the county. The Nature Conservancy has helped purchase several key components of the MSCP habitat network on behalf of San Diego County. Although the MSCP is still incomplete, its prospects look bright. Once the common wisdom was that human and wildlife habitats were incompatible. Now planners and businessmen are realizing that protecting a region's environment actually benefits the region's economy. As one San Diego economist observed, "Habitat has become infrastructure."

While the MSCP focuses on the more urbanized western half of San Diego County, The Nature Conservancy is also formulating a strategy to conserve threatened landscapes across the wilder eastern side of the county. Here, amid rolling grasslands and creeks lined with towering oaks and sycamores, cattle-raising survives as a way of life—as do at least seventy-four species of plants and animals unique to the South Coast. The Conservancy's Eastern San Diego Mountains Project hopes to harmonize the vital interests of burrowing owls and hard-working ranchers. By purchasing some properties and obtaining conservation easements on others, the Conservancy is attempting to link major sections of Cleveland National Forest and Anza-Borrego Desert State Park. If this project succeeds, it will be a major step toward establishing a

Maurice Braun (1877-1941)
San Diego Countryside with River, c. 1925
oil on canvas, 30 x 40 inches
Private collection, courtesy of The Irvine Museum

Carl Oscar Borg (1879-1947)
Santa Barbara Coastline
oil on canvas, 24 x 30 inches
The Irvine Museum

Elmer Wachtel (1864-1929)
Santa Paula Valley
oil on canvas, 30 x 40 inches
The Irvine Museum

PRECEDING PAGES
Granville Redmond (1871-1935)
California Landscape with Flowers
oil on canvas, 32 x 80 inches
The Irvine Museum

network of nature reserves that stretches from the Sonoran Desert to the Pacific coast.

For those trying to save what remains of the South Coast's natural environment, huge challenges remain. In Los Angeles and Ventura counties, the Santa Monica Mountains Conservancy has been acquiring open space for twenty years. Most of that quasi-governmental agency's efforts have focused on the Santa Monica Mountains, a range of rugged hills slicing through the heart of Los Angeles. By 2025, the population of the Los Angeles region is projected to increase by 6 million—another two Chicagos. This flood of humanity threatens to isolate the Santa Monica Mountains, turning them into a biological island. The Nature Conservancy hopes to establish wildlife corridors that connect the Santa Monicas with the Santa Susana Mountains to the north while also preserving open space throughout the Santa Clara Valley, once an idyllic agricultural center that now faces heavy pressures from suburbanization.

Many experts believe southern California, with its huge economy and mushrooming population, spells the future for all urban centers. If so, the efforts of The Nature Conservancy and its partner organizations can serve as a model for any metropolitan region trying to maintain natural values in the face of explosive growth. While the days are long gone when a traveler could ride the South Coast's open trails for league upon league, southern California's native grandeur endures, and prospects for its long-term health may be brightening.

THE CENTRAL COAST

The Marriage of City and Country

Virgil Williams
(1830-1886)
*View South from
Sonoma Hills
toward San Pablo
Bay and Mount
Tamalpais, 1864*
oil on canvas,
30 x 48 inches
Private collection,
courtesy of the
Montgomery
Gallery,
San Francisco

EVERY FIFTY SECONDS, CALIFORNIA WELCOMES A NEW resident. Although many are born here, millions of others choose to follow a dream and immigrate. They make that pivotal life decision for diverse reasons. Some come for the climate. Others crave personal freedom. Many simply admire the beauty of the place. But by far, most immigrants head to California because they seek a better life.

In a state renowned for its landscapes *and* lifestyles, no region embodies the California dream better than the Central Coast, stretching from Marin County to San Luis Obispo County. Here a vibrant human economy is interwoven with vast landscapes of stunning natural beauty. Throw in some mild weather and a social atmosphere noted for tolerance, and you have a magnet that attracts people of all stripes, including the upscale, the downtrodden, the overachieving, and the undernourished. Most unpack their bags, settle in, and never leave.

Only a dozen miles separate the gleaming skyscrapers of San Francisco from the towering redwoods of Muir Woods. That juxtaposition is no anomaly. Throughout the San Francisco region, indeed the whole Central Coast, tremendous amounts of wildlands have been preserved. Almost everywhere you find plunging coastlines, forested slopes, vast marshlands. Small wonder that San Francisco is the most popular tourist city in the world. Paris is second.

A remarkably diverse climate characterizes the Central Coast. On summer days, wool-clad San Franciscans may be shivering through a foggy fifty degrees, and fifteen miles east, the mercury is pushing 100. Likewise, rainfall amounts vary wildly. The drier inland areas typically receive less than fifteen inches annually, while more than sixty inches drench the Santa Cruz Mountains.

Ransom Gillet Holdredge (1836-1899)
Scene in the Santa Cruz Mountains
oil on canvas, 48 x 30 inches
The Oakland Museum of California:
Gift of Mr. and Mrs. Fred A. Bacsik

The topography of the Central Coast dictates the climatic range. Except for a few gaps carved by rivers, mountains line the full length of the coast. Some peaks near Big Sur approach 6,000 feet. The coastal range catches most of the precipitation swept in from the Pacific, casting a rain shadow over the interior. On sunny days when the inland valleys heat up, air rises, drawing in fog and cool ocean air from the Pacific.

A tremendous variety of plants and animals thrives in this mosaic of microclimates. The coast redwood, *Sequoia sempervirens*, is commonly seen as the signature species of the Central Coast. Once decimated by logging, the redwood has rebounded and is now common throughout much of the region, particularly on damp north-facing slopes. Oaks too are characteristic of the landscape. Nine of California's eleven species of oak trees can be found along the Central Coast. Throughout the region, pockets of coastal dunes, sand hills, and other vanishing habitats provide homes for unusual plants, animals, and insects.

One reason so much open land has survived along the Central Coast is the region's long history of conservation. Perhaps this ethic first set roots the day John Muir stepped off a steamer in San Francisco in 1868. When asked where he was heading, the exuberant Scotsman replied, "Anywhere that is wild!"

Muir established his reputation as champion of the Sierra Nevada, but for decades he lived in the Bay Area. In 1892, Muir founded the Sierra Club. Its aggressive defense of wild country has been especially effective along California's Central Coast. But the Sierra Club does not toil here alone. Thousands of individuals and hundreds of organizations have followed in the footsteps of John Muir. *Harper's* once sarcastically observed that nature "was practically *invented* in the San Francisco Bay area."

Edward A. Simmons (1852-1931)
*The Bosom of the Land, San Anselmo,
California*, 1914
oil on canvas, 24 x 24 inches
Courtesy of the Garzoli Gallery,
San Rafael

In 1934, in the midst of the great Depression, citizens of Alameda County voted to tax themselves to preserve 10,000 acres of land in the East Bay hills. Over the decades that original purchase has grown eight-fold. Now every municipality in Alameda and neighboring Contra Costa County contributes to the East Bay Regional Park District (EBRPD), the nation's first regional park authority. Inland, EBRPD's large wilderness parks span remote valleys, while closer to the coast, the park authority protects more than thirty miles of undeveloped hills that separate the cities along San Francisco Bay from the burgeoning suburbs to the east. Within minutes the two million residents of Alameda and Contra Costa counties can be strolling through oak and bay woodlands, tiptoeing through ferns and redwoods, or gazing over grasslands ablaze with lupine. Climb many of the higher peaks in the East Bay and you see San Francisco to the west, shimmering like Oz. Look behind you, and ridge after ridge of open land stretches into the distance, defying the fact that you stand in the middle of the nation's fifth-largest metropolitan area.

Mount Diablo: Inspiration, Refuge, and Heritage

I HAVE LIVED IN THE SHADOW of Mount Diablo for most of my life. As a boy, in the 1940s and early 1950s, I played in its foothills. I saw those hills transformed by residential home development during the post-war housing boom in Contra Costa County. At the dawn of the twenty-first century, Diablo stands as a silent sentinel, reminding us of a time when civilization had not advanced into rural California. Today, when I walk on the mountain, alone or with my children and friends, I often think of that time earlier in this century when Diablo was first beginning to feel the effects of an advancing urban culture. Two of my ancestors were participants in that process, representing two widely different perspectives.

My imaginings during Diablo walks take many and varied forms. In one day-dream, I imagine I can hear my maternal grandfather, Robert Noble Burgess, as he wove a convincing story to William Randolph Hearst on an afternoon horseback ride they took to the summit sometime in 1913. My grandfather, a real estate developer who, for a time, owned a considerable amount of the mountain, includ-ing the summit, was proposing to Hearst that the two collaborate in a business venture, and create summer homes in an area encompassing today's town of Diablo. Hearst was interested, and committed to a partnership in which he would employ the power of his newspaper chain to promote the venture throughout the country and my grandfather would build and sell the homes. History overtook the project in 1917, however, when the country was swept into World War I.

Sixteen years later, another relative, my paternal great-uncle, also played a role in the history of the mountain. Serving as Governor of California, James Rolph Jr. ("Sunny Jim") presided over the ceremony in which Mount Diablo was rededicated as a State Park in April 1931. Rolph's role was to act as the protector of the interests of all Californians, insuring that the land would be forever reserved for its aesthetic and recreational qualities.

Enhanced by this historic perspective, Mount Diablo has significant personal meaning for me. First and foremost, it is a refuge from the cares of an increasingly complicated world, providing solace and peace during long walks in all seasons of the year. It represents stability in a sea of change, which, to this rather mature observer, does not always seem to be for the best. Finally, personified by the involvement of forebears many decades earlier, Mount Diablo symbolizes the two conflicting themes of development and preservation.

JAMES R. MOORE, JR., *fourth-generation Californian*

Norton Bush (1834-1894)
Mount Diablo
oil on canvas, 20 x 16 inches
Private collection, courtesy of the North Point Gallery, San Francisco

In 1959, Catherine Kerr, wife of the president of the University of California, read a newspaper report outlining a U.S. Army Corps of Engineers plan to fill most of San Francisco Bay. Concerned, she teamed with two other faculty wives to form a grassroots organization that eventually persuaded the California legislature to institute the San Francisco Bay Conservation and Development Commission, the nation's first coastal management agency. Today that agency has virtually halted all filling of the bay. Though three-fourths of the bay's original wetlands are lost, seventy-five square miles remain, constituting one of the largest

Julian Rix (1851-1903)
Foggy Morning, Near San Rafael, 1881
oil on canvas, 20 x 36 inches
Crocker Art Museum, Sacramento
Purchased with funds from the Maude T. Pool Fund

Estero

DAWN. I SIT ON A BOULDER near the mouth of a shallow embayment, *Limantour Estero*, one of those places where the natural and the mythic landscapes overlap. The tide has soused the estuary with cold water upwelled from the California current. Fog shrouds the bay, so the flocks of birds that forage at the edge of the incoming tide are invisible, but their voices are amplified by the moisture—insistent tattles of godwits and willets, the braying of brant, eerie whistles of wigeon. Bat rays and leopard sharks glide in silent on the flood tide and forage across the tidal flats, snipping off siphons of razor clams and geoducks. At the bottom of the chalky cliffs is a cobbled beach where brittle stars, anemones, and barnacles abound. Shore crabs scuttle through crevices and crannies in the cobble. Over the years limpets and abalone have been mostly picked clean by intrepid hikers, but still, the rocky shore seethes with multitudes of invertebrates busy running the world.

If this misty *estero* isn't primordial, nowhere is.

As the fog begins to lift, I see across the inlet a twisted root of a coyote bush that protrudes from the cliff face . . . the peregrine falcon's favored perch. There the tercel roosts, plucking a bufflehead duck deliberately, as deliberately as a grandmother darning socks. As the duck's downy breast feathers drift off through the air, down toward the water, a swallow swoops and catches a single white feather in its beak. Three deer pick their path down a steep slope. A raven patrols the tideline for shorecast carrion—carcasses of bird and fish or other sealife tangled in the tidal wrack. Eelgrass blades bend on the slackening tide. All are making the world, much the way coyote made the world a long time ago.

JULES EVENS
naturalist and author of
The Natural History of the Point Reyes Peninsula

salt marsh complexes in the United States. That acreage is growing as conservation organizations resurrect salt marshes from pastures, salt farms, and even some industrial sites. The process is simple: just add water. Breach the levees and the tides do the rest.

In 1579, Sir Francis Drake, the first European visitor to California, is believed to have anchored in a sheltered bay along Point Reyes in Marin County. If the great navigator and part-time pirate were alive today, he would find that bay—in fact the entire coastline of Point Reyes—largely unchanged. Almost the whole western half of Marin— over 200 square miles—is composed of cliff-lined beaches, estuaries, lagoons, grasslands, and woods of fir and pine or maple and oak. The bugle of elk ringing through fog is a familiar sound to hikers on Point Reyes, while bird-watchers standing on a hilltop just miles from downtown San Francisco can study the nation's greatest concentration of migratory hawks.

A few Marin preserves such as Mount Tamalpais State Park and Muir Woods National Monument date back to the early twentieth century, but most of the county's breathtaking landscapes were set aside more recently. Responding to advocacy groups like the Sierra Club, Congress authorized the Point Reyes National Seashore in 1962 and a decade later funded the Golden Gate National Recreation Area (GGNRA), now the largest urban park in the world. The Nature Conservancy assisted in the birth of the GGNRA by purchasing the Gerbode Valley, preventing the owner of the property from developing a new city that would have hammered a wedge into the wildlands of Marin. A few years later, the Conservancy transferred the Gerbode Valley to the National Park Service.

While a remarkable forty-four percent of Marin County is publicly accessible park land, the Marin Agricultural Land Trust (MALT)

Preserving Bolinas Lagoon, Tomales Bay, and the Wild and Scenic Rivers of the North Coast

AS A BOY SCOUT GROWING UP in the sprawling port city of Oakland before World War II, I'd take the ferry to Sausalito, transfer to the electric train to Mill Valley, and hike across the mountain to camp near Bolinas Lagoon.

I idolized the salt-scented baylands, lagoons and coastline of Marin County, where great flights of sea birds shimmered like necklaces in the sky. I worshipped Mount Tamalpais looming above the fog, guarding California's virgin treasure, the gravel-bedded, undammed rivers of the Coast. Here I had fished with my father in crystal waters teeming with silver salmon and steelhead, and drifted silently down wild rivers through forests draped with golden wild grape.

After starting my medical practice in Marin after the war, I was angered to see the Bolinas Lagoon ringed with burning garbage dumps. In 1958, Gov. Pat Brown had promised to build a thousand miles of free-way and dam every wild river on the North Coast for water export to the south. In response, I organized my patients, medical friends, and the tiny Marin Audubon Society to create the Audubon Canyon Ranch wildlife sanctuaries. Over eleven years, we raised millions of dollars to save the egret heronry and habitats of Bolinas Lagoon and Tomales Bay, buying back public tidelands sold to developers at state auction in the 1860s. The battle spread to help save Tomales Bay, the Point Reyes National Seashore, Marin County itself, the Russian River, and, in 1972, the Wild and Scenic Rivers—Eel, Klamath, Trinity, and Smith.

My favorite battle—for the Bolinas Lagoon—was won with the help of TheNature Conservancy in 1967. The Bolinas Harbor District was moving ahead with plans to dredge the Lagoon for a 1,200-boat marina on Kent Island. In the nick of time, I obtained an option from the owners, and with the Conservancy, we presented it as a gift to Marin County—killing the marina, sinking the coastal freeway, and ending development planned for 150,000 people in the Bolinas Basin and on the east shore of Tomales Bay.

This is why you can travel far north from teeming San Francisco along a wild coast unblemished by freeway or housing tracts.

MARTIN GRIFFIN, M.D.
author, Saving the Marin-Sonoma Coast

Raymond Dabb Yelland
(1848-1900)
Summer Morn, Los Gatos, 1880
oil on canvas, 28 x 48 inches
Courtesy of the Garzoli Gallery,
San Rafael

has focused on preserving another component of Marin's open space: farms. Usually MALT pursues this aim by purchasing agricultural easements, which permanently exclude any use of a property that diminishes its agricultural value. The nation's first agricultural land trust, MALT has secured easements on 27,000 acres of Marin County farmland.

On the San Francisco Peninsula, the conservation story is equally compelling. Head south along the western shore, and you wind along sixty miles of rocky coastline lying at the base of steep mountains. Redwoods cloak the higher slopes, while ranchlands and vegetable farms blanket the coastal terraces. On the eastern shore of the Peninsula, the businesses of Silicon Valley are transforming the American economy, but the wealth they generate has so inflated the local real estate market that it is now the most expensive in the United States. Nonetheless, organizations like the Midpeninsula Open Space District, the Peninsula Open Space Trust, the Save the Redwoods League, and the Trust for Public Land have successfully preserved much of the dramatic natural landscape that stretches from San Francisco to Santa Cruz. These organizations are regularly acquiring additional large tracts, tightening the green belt that makes Silicon Valley a pleasing place to live and work while simultaneously ensuring the integrity of the natural communities of the coastal mountains.

At the extreme southern end of San Francisco Bay, the goals are much the same for The Nature Conservancy's Mount Hamilton project. Here subdivisions and office parks are galloping south from San Jose, while across the nearby Diablo Range, the Modesto region is also suburbanizing with gut-wrenching speed. "Our Mount Hamilton project," says Steve McCormick, former executive director of the Conservancy's California chapter, "will protect critical habitats and open spaces between two rapidly growing areas: the Silicon Valley and the Central Valley." Along with a partner organization, the Santa Clara County Open Space Authority, The Nature Conservancy has purchased three large ranches totaling 70,000 acres, guaranteeing that the citizens of San Jose will always see an open horizon to the south.

The Mount Hamilton acquisitions are home to rare alluvial sycamore woodlands and five types of oak, including both valley and blue oak, unique to California and disappearing throughout much of the state. Species as disparate as the tule elk and the Bay checkerspot butterfly frequent the area. Eventually, the Conservancy plans to transfer some

Franz Bischoff (1864-1929)
Monterey Farm
oil on board, 13 x 18 inches
The Irvine Museum

The Road to Silver Creek Valley

I GREW UP IN THE FOOTHILLS of the Santa Clara Valley, in early days known as the Valley of Heart's Delight. When I was a child, nearly every weekend my father would take us to the ranch, an expanse of oak woodland across the valley in the Diablo Range. We'd drive east through the orchards and towns, then turn up a winding valley on Silver Creek Road. It was here that we entered another world—the valley oak woodlands. The huge trees towered over the grassy hillsides, each one like a giant sculpture. The narrow creek valley itself was shaded with thick stands of sycamores, buckeyes, and bay trees. In the spring, wildflowers were scattered under the oaks like jewels. The name Silver Creek Valley seemed perfect to me for a road to a magical and precious place.

Today that entire valley is laid bare, scraped clean, and covered with thousands of homes. California's natural heritage is nothing less than remarkable, a story of superlatives on all accounts—amazing habitat diversity, huge numbers of endemic species, and some of the most beautiful landscapes in North America. We're losing this heritage, and with it, not only the wildlife and watersheds, the ecosystem services, and the resources that benefit humankind. We're losing the opportunity to create thousands of childhood experiences in nature. For me, these were the inspiration for my life passion for conservation. It's our responsibility to protect these habitats for the next generations, so that they, too, can be inspired to be stewards of this remarkable place for the future.

JULIE PACKARD, *Director, Monterey Bay Aquarium*

Mount Hamilton properties to local authorities for use as public parks. On others, ranching operations will continue, preserving a way of life that itself is becoming endangered throughout much of California.

Not only the Bay Area can boast of many conservation successes; the whole Central Coast is similarly blessed. Along Monterey Bay, The Nature Conservancy has been active since the 1960s, when it began acquiring Elkhorn Slough, the largest estuary in the state after San Francisco Bay. Estuaries form where fresh and salt water intermingle, creating some of the most biologically productive habitat in the world. Landfill and other human activities have destroyed ninety percent of California's estuarine environments. Elkhorn Slough reminds us of what has been lost. Paddle a kayak along its winding tidal creeks and you pass egrets, avocets, black-necked stilts. You might even spot an endangered California clapper rail. A breeding ground for many marine species, Elkhorn Slough serves as a vital link between land-based ecosystems and 5,000 square miles of open ocean protected by the Monterey Bay National Marine Sanctuary.

Guy Rose (1867-1925)
Carmel Seascape
oil on canvas, 21 x 24 inches
Private collection, courtesy of The Irvine Museum

ARTHUR HILL GILBERT.

Arthur Hill Gilbert
(1894-1970)
Land Of Grey Dunes,
Monterey
oil on canvas, 32 x 40 inches
The Irvine Museum

William Wendt (1865-1946)
The Soil (Near San Luis Obispo)
oil on canvas, 30 x 36 inches
Private collection, courtesy of
The Irvine Museum

Farther south, The Nature Conservancy has been actively preserving another piece of California's natural heritage, the Guadalupe-Nipomo Dunes. This intricate patchwork of private and public lands constitutes the largest, most ecologically complex sand dune system in California, including the tallest dunes in the state, some 500 feet tall. Eighteen rare species of plants grow here. Seasonal wildflowers like dune larkspur and Indian paintbrush splash color over the landscape. More than 200 species of birds live or migrate through the dunes.

To ensure the viability of a nature preserve, you need friendly neighbors. The Nature Conservancy has made a special effort to incorporate the Guadalupe-Nipomo Dunes into the local community. The Conservancy has recruited local volunteers, sponsored a variety of school programs and adult education opportunities, and established a discovery center for visitors. In 1998 that center featured a curious exhibit: a celebration of the set for Cecil B. DeMille's 1923 silent epic *The Ten Commandments*. After the movie was filmed here, its lavish

backdrops, replete with sphinxes and pharaonic statues, were abandoned and eventually lost beneath the shifting sands of the Guadalupe-Nipomo Dunes. Film buffs rediscovered them in the 1980s.

Recently, The Nature Conservancy launched an initiative to protect natural areas throughout San Luis Obispo County. Operating with funding from The David and Lucile Packard Foundation, the Conservancy is working with its local partners to identify landscapes that possess outstanding biological, scenic, and agricultural values. Efforts to conserve land have begun in the Irish Hills and Indian Knob areas of the coastal range, in the oak woodlands south of Atascadero, and in the Monterey pine forests near Cambria.

At the southeastern end of San Luis Obispo County, The Nature Conservancy is completing one of its most successful long-term projects: the Carrizo Plain Natural Area. Here the Conservancy has worked with the U.S. Bureau of Land Management and the California Department of Fish and Game to conserve a quarter million acres of this vast and isolated basin, sandwiched between the Temblor and Caliente Ranges and straddling the relentless and clearly visible San Andreas Fault.

Modernity has mostly overlooked the Carrizo. Over the decades, many hucksters have tried to peddle property here to gullible buyers, packaging these arid grasslands in various forms—a vacation destination, a fertile ground for cultivating jojoba, an aviation-based community. The Carrizo has thwarted all such mendacity. It is simply too dry, too remote.

Today, cattle ranching sustains the sparse human population—just as it has for 100 years—while a web of unusual and largely intact ecosystems support the largest collection of rare animals found anywhere in the nation. Look closely, and if you're lucky, you might spot a San Joaquin kit fox, a giant kangaroo rat, a blunt-nosed leopard lizard, or a San Joaquin antelope squirrel. Recently, the newly reintroduced California condor has been paying visits.

Historically, tule elk and pronghorn antelope lived in this valley, but both were extirpated long ago—the last pronghorn shot in 1912. In the late 1980s, after years of planning, the California Department of Fish and Game reintroduced both species. Jim Lidberg, who managed the state program, described seeing those pronghorn shoot out of a holding pen and rocket across the plain. "It was one of the high points of my career, the culmination of ten years of planning. I never thought I'd live to see it." According to Lidberg, the sight of pronghorn bounding across the Carrizo brought tears to the eyes of gruff old-timers.

Today, the elk are flourishing, and more than 600 antelope roam "California's Serengeti," as the Carrizo has recently been dubbed. Viewing its role on the Carrizo as nearly complete, The Nature Conservancy has transferred most of its property to the Bureau of Land Management. The federal government is now considering National Monument status for the Carrizo Plain.

Many people believe that an expanding human population cannot coexist with large, relatively pristine natural landscapes. Certainly the explosive growth of California has extracted a terrible toll on the state's natural heritage. But the Central Coast belies many of those worries. Although ten or more new residents arrived in the state during the time you spent reading this chapter, if those newcomers live along the Central Coast, there's a fair chance a few may follow the lead of John Muir and dedicate themselves to keeping the natural landscapes of California forever wild.

Albert Derome (1885-1959)
Purple Bush Lupine,
Salinas Canyon
oil on board, 18 x 23-1/2 inches
Private collection, courtesy of
The Irvine Museum

THE DESERT

A String of Pearls

THROUGHOUT MUCH OF CALIFORNIA'S HISTORY, THE DESERT has been a place reviled. Anyone unfortunate enough to cross one of California's barren wastelands prayed to complete the journey safely. Only prospectors, cranks, outlaws, and mystics willingly chose to live amid the desolation of the desert.

Over the last few decades, however, attitudes have changed. Thanks in large part to aqueducts and air conditioning, the desert is now accessible—even desirable. Every weekend armies of recreation-seekers, ranging from birdwatchers to off-road motorcyclists, descend on the austere and fragile landscape that stretches from Death Valley to the Mexican border.

In some parts of the California desert, especially the Coachella Valley around Palm Springs, people are not just visiting—they're homesteading. Long a favorite retreat for the Hollywood set, Palm Springs has transformed the golf course and the Rolls Royce into symbols of desert life. The image sells so well, the population of the Coachella Valley has swollen from 12,000 in 1940 to a quarter million today. Some now say the desert is being loved to death.

Few places on earth can match the beauty and diversity of California's deserts. East of the Sierra Nevada stretches the Great Basin, a landscape of steep, high mountain ranges separated by deep troughs, most notably Death Valley with its otherworldly salt flats and sand dunes. Some of the steepest elevation changes on the continent occur here. Less than a hundred miles separate White Mountain Peak, over 14,000 feet high, from Badwater, nearly 300 feet below sea level.

Farther south lies the Mojave Desert, called the high desert because its elevation never dips below 1,000 feet. Stretching from the northern suburbs of Los Angeles to the Nevada state line, the Mojave is

Gordon Coutts
(1868-1937)
*End of
the Day*
oil on canvas,
20 x 30 inches
The Irvine
Museum

John Frost (1890-1937)
Devil's Playground
oil on canvas, 26 x 30 inches
Private collection,
courtesy of The Irvine Museum

home to rugged mountain ranges, dry lake beds, and top-secret military reservations. Every year thousands of visitors scramble over the sculpted sienna boulders of Joshua Tree National Park or launch forays into the remote canyons, basins, and creosote flats of the Mojave National Preserve, created under the 1994 California Desert Protection Act.

Head even farther south and you descend into the low desert, the Colorado Desert, hotter in the summer and milder in the winter than the Mojave. Extending from eastern Riverside County to the Colorado River, the Colorado Desert is part of the greater Sonoran Desert, which spans much of Arizona and northern Mexico. Less remote than the Mojave, the low desert includes the densely settled Coachella Valley, the heavily cultivated Imperial Valley, and the Salton Sea, formed in 1905 when flooding on the Colorado and Gila Rivers broke through the Imperial Valley's irrigation system, diverting water into a low-lying basin. A region known for its fan palms, smoke trees, and sand dunes (as well as its swimming pools and putting greens), the low desert comprises many strikingly beautiful natural areas, such as Anza-Borrego Desert State Park, California's largest state park. Anza-Borrego annually boasts one of the West's most spectacular wildflower displays.

Harsh weather underlies much of the desert's beauty—and mystery. Precipitation can be incredibly sparse. El Centro, near the Mexican border, receives only three-quarters of an inch annually. With no water vapor to buffer temperatures, the thermometer fluctuates wildly, often from one hour to the next. In the Mojave, daily swings of eighty degrees are common. Because the desert air is so dry, however, it has a crystalline quality. Shadows are deep, colors vivid. Familiar landscapes seem to change texture and hue as the sun plays over them. When rains do come, they can be torrential, scouring canyons and flooding dry lake beds.

Within hours after a storm, carpets of wildflowers can erupt into bloom, transforming the parched desert floor into a storybook fantasy.

The plants and animals adapted to these hostile conditions can seem exotic. The Joshua tree, a characteristic species of the high desert, looks like something you might see scuba diving. Technically, it is not a tree at all but a member of the yucca family. The chuckwalla, a large desert lizard, can wedge itself into rocky crevices by inflating its body—a novel defense mechanism. The Coachella Valley fringe-toed lizard can actually *swim under* sand. When surface temperatures grow too extreme or a predator appears, the sandswimmer, as the fringe-toed lizard is sometimes called, dives beneath the sand in a flick of the eye. It can stay submerged indefinitely, breathing the air trapped between sand grains.

To survive, the fringe-toed lizard depends on a steady supply of loose, fine-grained sand, known locally as blowsand. Rainstorms wash sand down the mountain canyons, and then the constant desert winds shape it into dunes that move as much as several feet a day. Barriers of any sort, natural or man-made, restrict the flow of blowsand. In the 1980s plenty of barriers were springing up—like luxury hotels and condominiums. Recognizing the precarious ecological position of the fringe-toed lizard, biologists successfully petitioned state and federal governments to declare the sandswimmer endangered. Soon the U. S. Fish and Wildlife Service was threatening to halt construction throughout the Coachella Valley—a move that would have cost developers billions of dollars.

Battle lines formed. After some rancorous confrontations, builders and environmentalists realized they faced a stalemate. The developers lost money every day their projects were delayed, but the fringe-toed

Jean Mannheim (1862-1945)
By the Salton Sea
oil on masonite, 20 x 24 inches
Courtesy of DeRu's Fine Arts,
Laguna Beach

lizard was losing its grip on life as its habitat steadily streamed away. Hoping a trusted third party could broker an agreement, the deadlocked factions turned to The Nature Conservancy.

Basing its actions on a clause in the federal Endangered Species Act, the Conservancy helped forge a plan for developers and government agencies to pay for the creation of a nature reserve. It would be large enough to ensure the survival of the fringe-toed lizard, and it would include the artesian springs and palm forest at the beautiful Thousand Palms oasis.

Paul T. Selzer, a lawyer instrumental in forming the plan, said, "It was the most fulfilling role I've ever played as an attorney. It convinced me there are techniques that you can use to bring warring factions together." The Nature Conservancy contributed $2 million for purchasing property, directed land acquisitions, and for years managed the resulting Coachella Valley Preserve. In 1997 the Conservancy handed over authority for the preserve to the Center for Natural Lands Management, an organization that specializes in stewardship of conservation lands. Now, 40,000 people a year visit the preserve, lingering in the shade of the trees and listening to the rustling palm fronds, or strolling the dunes and watching the wind sculpt the ever-shifting sand.

The Coachella Valley agreement stands as a landmark in conservation history. It was one of the first efforts to preserve a species' complete habitat under the auspices of the Endangered Species Act, and it pioneered the technique of facilitating cooperation among disparate interests. That notion formed the basis of California's Natural Communities Conservation Planning program, which successfully defused the Orange County crisis over the California gnatcatcher (see page 29).

Some compromises struck during the Coachella Valley negotiations have resulted in unexpected long-term problems. In particular, the source of the blowsand was never protected. Now real estate development threatens to sever the connection between the Indio Hills, the main sand source, and the Coachella Valley Preserve. Once again biologists, developers, and government officials have come to the bargaining table, hoping to devise an even more comprehensive habitat plan. Dubbed the Coachella Valley Multiple Species Habitat Conservation Plan, this effort could guarantee the survival of a cluster of precious natural sites surrounding the Coachella Valley—"a string of pearls," according to Ed Hastey, former California director of the U.S. Bureau of Land Management.

"These sites are jewels in every sense of the word," says Cameron Barrows, Southern California Regional Director for the Center for Natural Lands Management. "They hold the last remnants of this area's biological heritage." In recent years The Nature Conservancy has worked with its local partners to secure many of these pearls and to string them together by protecting the natural processes—like sand corridors—that connect them.

Twenty miles north of Palm Springs lies the Morongo Valley, dividing the San Bernardino Mountains from the Little San Bernardinos. Big Morongo Canyon begins in the Mojave and ends in the Colorado Desert. For centuries Native Americans used this natural highway between high desert and low. Water was available and game plentiful. The last people to inhabit the canyon before the advent of white settlers were the Morongos, a clan of the Serrano Indians.

Unlike most valleys in the world, here streams run at right angles to the prevailing topography. Rain that falls in the San Bernardino Mountains flows underground along geologic fault lines until it rises to the surface in the Morongo Valley. The largest stream, Big Morongo Creek, forms a rare desert marsh. A profusion of life responds to the presence of water in Big Morongo Canyon. Great cottonwoods loom overhead. Willow and mesquite choke the water's edge.

At Big Morongo, coastal climate patterns influence the intersection between high and low desert habitat, resulting in what biologists call an

Paul Grimm
(1892-1974)
Desert Springs
oil on board, 24 x 18 inches
Private collection, courtesy of
The Irvine Museum

Paul Grimm
(1892-1974)
Palm Canyon
oil on board,
20 x 24 inches
Private collection,
courtesy of
The Irvine Museum

Paul Grimm (1892-1974)
Desert Scene
oil on board, 12 x 16 inches
Private collection,
courtesy of
The Irvine Museum

ecotone—a transitional area between adjacent ecological communities. Ecotones typically produce great biological diversity, and Big Morongo Canyon is no exception. It has more flora and fauna than any oasis in the Mojave, including 270 bird species.

Sit quietly at dawn or dusk and you might see deer, bobcats, or desert bighorn sheep descending to the valley floor in search of water. Do your wildlife spotting in autumn, and you might be lucky enough to spy on bighorn rams as they establish their dominance hierarchies. The rams work out their differences in a straightforward manner: they butt heads at speeds up to forty-five miles an hour.

The Nature Conservancy became involved at Big Morongo in 1968 after receiving a gift of land, a strategically located parcel at the canyon's mouth. For years the Conservancy administered the site, but recently the Bureau of Land Management, which holds almost 4,000 adjoining acres, assumed management. The Nature Conservancy remains involved in an advisory role.

Another pearl on the string of low desert landscapes is the Mission Creek watershed, which connects Big Morongo to the San Bernardino National Forest and the Coachella Valley. Mountain brooks descending from high in the San Bernardino Mountains form the headwaters of Mission Creek. Like Big Morongo Canyon, Mission Creek is a biologically rich intersection between high desert, low desert, and coastal climate patterns.

The story of how Mission Creek was protected illustrates the range of strategies The Nature Conservancy will sometimes use to preserve land, often at minimal cost. For one Mission Creek parcel, the Conservancy traded a property in Los Angeles County because the L.A. land provided its owners with a better return on investment. For another 1,200 acres, the Conservancy promised the owners a monthly annuity. After receiving the property, the Conservancy resold it to the California Department of Fish and Game. Proceeds from the sale fund the annuity. Most of the land at Mission Creek, 2,400 acres, was a gift from the McKesson Corporation (recently acquired by the French Groupe

Paul Grimm (1892-1974)
Cumulus Clouds
oil on canvas, 28 x 36 inches
Private collection, courtesy of The Irvine Museum

Paul Grimm
(1892-1974)
Stately Palms
oil on canvas,
20 x 24 inches
Private collection,
courtesy of
The Irvine Museum

Danone S.A.). Charles A. Norris, President of McKesson, said, "We knew that by donating this land to the Conservancy, we would be protecting it from development and keeping it pristine for future generations." Once Mission Creek seemed destined for a fate similar to much of the Coachella Valley's. Riverside County had already approved the McKesson site for condominiums, a hotel, and a golf course. Now it is prowled by mountain lions, rather than men chasing little white balls.

Heading southeast from the Coachella Valley, you pass miles of sand and scraggly brush until a splash of green appears on the horizon. The Dos Palmas oasis seems like a vision, a breath of life in an otherwise lifeless landscape. Here hundreds of desert fan palms—the only palm tree native to the western United States—circle artesian springs. Cattails line the water's edge.

The waters of Dos Palmas originally attracted the Cahuilla Indians, who lived at the oasis for centuries. In the 1860s, Dos Palmas was a stop on the stagecoach line connecting Los Angeles to gold mines in western Arizona. During World War II, General George S. Patton trained troops not far from here before invading North Africa.

Today, Dos Palmas hosts hundreds of thousands of migrating birds. Rare species like the Yuma clapper rail, the black rail, and the prairie falcon make their homes at the oasis. The most unusual resident may be the desert pupfish. A relic of the Pleistocene era, the tiny pupfish—barely three inches long—is another miracle of adaptation. It

See the Desert with a Different Eye

THE DESERT IS NOT as easy to appreciate quickly as the ocean, forest, or meadow glen. To the uninitiated, it is dry, hot, empty, and lonely. It is something to avoid or get through as quickly as possible. It spells danger and conjures visions of death by heat exhaustion or thirst. For some, it is merely a big sandbox whose only worth is the space it provides for heedless recreational activity. For others, its worth is the sun—if tamed by water, air conditioning, modern conveniences, and golf courses.

There is something more to the desert, if one would clearly see. The desert can capture your very soul, or perhaps it is a door to your soul. It is that which has attracted the saints to the desert for thousands of years in search of God and themselves. It is not just the sense of timelessness, the vastness, the quiet, the changing moods that can tap your very being. It is what is hidden and takes time to see—the abundance and depth of life within the apparent emptiness; the will, determination and creativity to survive heat, drought and seasonal flash floods in innumerable adaptive ways; the fragility within its outward strength; and the glorious inner clock that signals to plants and animals that conditions are right for that burst of activity that can result in an incredible display of desert life among rock and sand. The desert does not easily share its secrets. It is reserved for the patient, the observant, and those who treat the desert with respect.

Time is running out for the desert. It has been discovered. Its gifts of sunshine and health call strongly to desert developers and recreationalists. The very space that makes it attractive is shrinking in a process that threatens to destroy wildlife and plants dependent on that space—the Peninsular desert bighorn sheep, the flat-tailed horned lizard, the desert pupfish, the southwest willow flycatcher, the least Bell's vireo, and the spectacular annual wildflower displays. Scientists are only beginning to understand the intricate and delicate relationships found in desert ecology. It is one of the most diverse landscapes and yet one of the most fragile because of its inability to recover quickly from intrusions.

The hope is in the hands of those whose understanding goes beyond immediate gratification. It is in the hands of caring individuals who will take a leap of faith that saving the desert in its pristine form is saving our own humanity. It is saving a place for the soul to take retreat. It is saving ourselves.

DIANA LINDSAY, *ecologist, Anza-Borrego Foundation*

Paul Grimm (1892-1974)
Desert Flowers
oil on board, 12 x 16 inches
Private collection, courtesy
of The Irvine Museum

can tolerate salinity levels three times as high as the ocean and water temperatures that vary fifty or sixty degrees in a day. Once found throughout the watersheds of the lower Colorado River, the pupfish has lost most of its habitat and is now a federally endangered species.

Recognizing the environmental significance of Dos Palmas, The Nature Conservancy began buying property here in 1989. Joining forces with the Bureau of Land Management and Ducks Unlimited, the Conservancy has worked to restore the fragile habitat of Dos Palmas. Teams from the Los Angeles Conservation Corps manually removed tamarisk, a non-native shrub. Left unchecked, tamarisk would have eventually consumed virtually all surface water at the oasis. Conservancy stewards eliminated exotic fish species that threatened the survival of the desert pupfish, and they recontoured ponds once used for fish farming. The new design creates a mosaic of sloughs, marshes, and islands that balances habitat for waterfowl, migratory birds, the pupfish, and other wildlife. Now the Conservancy is turning over management of Dos Palmas to the Center for Natural Lands Management. Describing The Nature Conservancy's achievements throughout the low desert, Cameron Barrows says, "None of this would have happened without The Nature Conservancy being the conservation catalyst."

Today, the once-common image of the California desert as a barren wasteland has mostly vanished from the public consciousness. This land of green palms and blue mountains holds a powerful allure for millions of Californians. No matter how people express their appreciation for the desert, most are responding to the same fundamental qualities— clear air, rainbow landscapes, and empty places to fill with their own thoughts, whether they be focused on chip shots or chuckwallas. The Nature Conservancy is working to preserve that precious heritage so future generations will know the meaning of a desert landscape.

THE GREAT CENTRAL VALLEY

Restoring a Bountiful Land

"THE RAINS CONTINUE, AND SINCE I LAST WROTE THE floods have been far worse than before. Sacramento and many other towns and cities have again been overflowed, and after the waters had abated somewhat they are again up. That doomed city is in all probability under water today." So wrote William H. Brewer, field leader of the first California Geological Survey, in an 1862 letter.

Despite Brewer's dire assessment, Sacramento survived the winter of 1862, the wettest in California history, and has persevered through many subsequent floods as well. To provide a measure of safety for the state capital and the rest of the Great Central Valley, Californians have erected one of the world's most elaborate hydrologic systems, including 1,200 dams and 1,800 miles of levees.

That flood control apparatus is just one of the wholesale environmental changes unleashed on the Central Valley in the name of progress. Here betterment comes at a high price, especially for the grizzly bear, the tule elk, the Chinook salmon, and a host of other vanished and vanishing species. But some environmental organizations like The Nature Conservancy see a different future for the Central Valley and, in places, are attempting to stop—even turn back—the hands of time.

The Central Valley is one of the flattest places on earth. Its distinguishing topographic feature is its lack of features. "The Valley," as residents call it, is a basin 400 miles long and fifty miles wide, rimmed by the Sierra Nevada to the east and the coast ranges to the west. Before the earth's tectonic motions thrust up those mountain chains, the Valley was an ancient seabed where, in places, sediments accumulated up to ten miles deep.

Two great rivers, the Sacramento in the north and the San Joaquin in the south, drain the Central Valley, although drainage is not a word

Tom Craig
(1909-1969)
California
oil on canvas,
24 x 36 inches
The Irvine
Museum

Eugen Neuhaus (1879-1963)
Sutter Buttes
oil on canvas, 30 x 40 inches
The Oakland Museum of California:
Gift of Mr. and Mrs. Robert Neuhaus

the first Europeans might have associated with the place. Early Spanish maps labeled the Valley *Cienegas de Tulares*, the tule swamps, after the bulrushes that flourish there on flooded lands. In fact, the prehistoric landscape of the Central Valley was more of a mosaic; grasslands and riparian forests intermingled with rivers, creeks, and marshes to form a landscape of remarkable natural wealth.

Migrating waterfowl blackened the sky. Early travelers sometimes encountered groups of thirty foraging grizzlies. Elk were said to be as abundant as the bison of the Great Plains. Three hundred tribes of Native Americans inhabited the Central Valley, and they lived in relative peace, thanks in part to the region's natural abundance.

Within decades after Father Junipero Serra led his expedition to San Francisco Bay in 1769, warfare and disease decimated the Native Americans, and hunters slaughtered the wildlife. By 1862, William Brewer recounted how elk "are now exterminated but we find their horns by the hundred." The first settlers raised cattle and sheep in the Central Valley, and soon the Eurasian weeds and grasses spread by livestock had almost wholly replaced the native bunchgrasses.

During the mid-nineteenth century, land use shifted to the cultivation of wheat and grains, and as irrigation became more feasible, farmers switched to orchard and row crops. Throughout the twentieth century, agricultural production skyrocketed. Today, the region grows more beets, peaches, grapes, walnuts, almonds, canteloupes, prunes, and tomatoes than any state in the country. Twenty-five percent of all table food eaten in the United States originates in the Central Valley.

In recent years, the Central Valley has been assuming yet another identity—urban center. Along the length of the Valley, cities like Bakersfield, Fresno, Modesto, Stockton, Yuba City, Marysville, Chico, and

The Sutter Buttes

THE SUTTER BUTTES ARE A FORMATION of craggy peaks and rolling hills in the Sacramento Valley. They rise about 2,000 feet above the floor of the Great Central Valley of California, and they are absolutely beautiful. They are a unique breach in the plain of the vast valley. Volcanic in origin, less than ten miles in diameter, they consist of three main peaks and are ringed with miniature foothills that form an almost circular boundary with the flatness of the valley. In the summer and autumn, they are golden, the color of California. In the winter, they are often shrouded in mists and clouds, giving them dark green and purple hues, and in the spring, they are verdant with new grass.

The Buttes were sacred to several tribes of Native Americans, among them the Wintun and the Maidu, who named them *Histum Yani* or Middle Mountains. Ironically, the American General, John C. Frémont, planned and led raids on tribal villages from his camp in the Buttes. His success in those skirmishes propelled him to his controversial and opportunistic involvement in the Bear Flag Revolt, the 1846 "rebellion" that led to events that wrested California from Mexico and paved the way for the flood of American and European immigrants to California.

My family arrived in the Sacramento Valley in the 1840s. They bought land about two miles south of the Buttes and settled there to ranch. When I was a child, I spent a significant part of my life there at my family's ranch. From my room I had a beautiful view of the Buttes. In my room in San Francisco hung a painting of the Buttes that my family had commissioned. As a result, most mornings of my childhood began with a view of the Buttes, and I became enthralled with their beauty on a very personal level. A trip into the Buttes for a picnic was always wonderful. I'll never forget the exhilaration of climbing a peak and looking across to the neighboring peak to see a golden eagle's nest with chicks whose parents were stooping and catching dinner for the family.

The Buttes are still undeveloped. They are privately owned, not a park or protected public land. So far, their natural beauty has been preserved by people who are, in effect, stewards of a great treasure. Most of the owners are local ranchers, as much of the privately owned open space in California is owned by people who make their living from agriculture. Without them, and the fruits of their labor, this open space would probably be developed. Hopefully the open space in California that has been preserved by agriculture will not succumb to development. Hopefully the people who own it will be encouraged to and allowed to keep it free of more asphalt, housing projects, office complexes and manufacturing plants. I hope that future generations of that family of eagles can soar over the Buttes and the Valley, and expanses of open space.

SCOTT LeFEVRE, *Californian*

William Smith Jewett
Hock Farm (A View of the Butte Mountains
from Feather River, California), 1851
oil on canvas, 28 x 39 inches
The Oakland Museum of California:
Gift of Anonymous Donor

Maynard Dixon (1875-1946)
Approaching Storm, 1921
oil on canvas, 26 x 20 inches
Fresno Metropolitan Museum

Sacramento have been paving over those ten-mile-deep sediments with strip malls and subdivisions. Forecasters predict that in forty years, a fifth of the Central Valley's agricultural land will be lost.

Unfortunately, the Central Valley's current priorities, agricultural production and residential development, often clash with a fundamental of fluid dynamics: Water in motion, whether it be a raindrop dribbling down a window or a river bearing steamships to the sea, tends to loop back and forth, to meander. In an effort to forestall this annoying fluvial tendency, California has straitjacketed all but one of the Central Valley's rivers, confining them to rectilinear channels lined with levees and faced with a rocky debris called riprap.

On New Year's Day of 1997, the rivers counterpunched. A warm, wet storm blew in from the Pacific, pounding the state with rain for five days and melting the Sierra snowpack. Flooding was catastrophic. The deluge inundated more land than any storm since the terrible winter of 1862. Months after the heaviest rains fell, 200,000 acres were still submerged, an area ten times the size of San Francisco.

"What do you do when the Sacramento River wants to wander into your back yard?" That is the question posed by Barney Flynn, who farms the west bank of the Sacramento ten miles downstream from Red Bluff. "We didn't invite it in, but twice in recent years the river came calling."

Farmers like Flynn are key to The Nature Conservancy's Sacramento River Project. Here the Conservancy aims to give 115 miles of limited freedom back to the Sacramento River, at the same time coaxing 33,000 acres of riparian land back to a state resembling what John Muir saw in 1868. Observing the mile-wide forests lining Central Valley rivers, Muir wrote that "along the water's edge there was a fine jungle of tropical luxuriance."

Joining forces with state and federal agencies, The Nature Conservancy has been purchasing flood-prone property along the Sacramento, often from farmers happy to shed a cash drain and a chronic headache. The Conservancy leases some of the land for agricultural purposes, usually to the farmer who sold it. On the remaining property, the

Conservancy and its partners have been attempting to resurrect the Central Valley's lush riparian forests.

In recent years, scientists have learned that revegetating riverbanks can be easy. Let the river level fluctuate normally, peaking in winter or spring, then gradually diminishing, and willows and cottonwood will voluntarily sprout on exposed gravel bars. Wildlife returns to the newborn thickets. Eventually, other types of trees establish themselves. In ten years a handsome stand of oak, ash, alder, and cottonwood may flourish where once there was only sand—or riprap.

This natural alchemy gets derailed if the water level drops too fast, typically the case downstream from dams. "The young trees get fried during the summer months," says Conservancy scientist Mike Roberts, "because the water is cut off too quickly." An alternative to natural reforestation is for humans to do the grunt work. Using mainstream agricultural methods, The Nature Conservancy is cultivating cottonwoods and sycamores as if they were almonds or tomatoes. Usually, the Conservancy hires the former landowner to perform any manual revegetation, giving the farmer and the local economy an infusion of cash. Once the trees get established, nature is allowed to reassert itself. Paddle a canoe down this stretch of the Sacramento a few years from now, and you may not recognize the hand of man for all the elderberry, snowberry, blackberry, mugwort, and wild grape. You might even mistake those river banks for a "jungle of tropical luxuriance."

Although restoration efforts along the Sacramento are only a few years old, some are already yielding results. Songbirds, including the yellow-billed cuckoo, have begun nesting in the restored habitat. Listed as an endangered species in California, the yellow-billed cuckoo is an indicator species: Its health reflects the health of the surrounding habitat. Once common in the streamside forests of the Central Valley, the cuckoo's numbers plunged as trees were felled and levees erected.

The Sacramento River Project does not just benefit wildlife. Giving the river room to sprawl relieves pressure on downstream levees during floods. And the riparian vegetation filters out silt and waterborne debris. After a flood, a farmer might have to spend up to $50,000 to remove debris and silt from a riverside project. So restoring streamside forests as natural buffers not only creates critical wildlife habitat, it also makes economic sense. Several years ago, the Conservancy had trouble persuading farmers to join the revegetation program. "Today," says Sam Lawson, manager of the Sacramento River Project, "we have to put some of the applicants on a waiting list."

In the southern half of the Central Valley, organizations are working to preserve and restore the region's environmental heritage. South of Fresno, the San Joaquin River Parkway and Conservation Trust is resurrecting riparian habitat along the San Joaquin River, much as the Conservancy is doing with its Sacramento River Project. Near Merced, the Conservancy is attempting to protect the world's largest expanse of unbroken vernal pool grasslands. The University of California has proposed a new campus for Merced, and if significant urban sprawl accompanies the new university, this unique landscape could be degraded. During the initial stages of the Merced Grasslands Project, the Conservancy is working with local organizations to acquire agricultural easements on key properties.

Twenty miles south of Sacramento flows the Cosumnes River, the Central Valley's last free-flowing river and site of The Nature Conservancy's Cosumnes River Preserve. Perhaps more than any Conservancy effort in California, the Cosumnes Preserve aims to protect a complete, functioning ecosystem.

Valley in Autumn

WELCOME TO MY VALLEY. Get off the freeway and wander through the country. Make sure to drive with the windows down— no matter the time of year. The complexity of sights and smells will introduce you to a Valley you otherwise might never have known existed.

Winter shrouds my Valley with sheets of thick tule fog and rain, spring is a riotous display of color and scent with almond, peach, and cherry blossoms as far as the eye can see, and summer brings varied harvests more bountiful than almost anywhere else in the world. But the Valley I love is best discovered during an autumn's drive.

In the autumn morning, the Valley floor still holds the heat from the previous day. Winter's approach is near, and the crisp air melds with the earth's heat to form a low-lying mist. When I allow myself to stand perfectly still for just a moment, this groundling mist envelops me in the musky undertones of yesterday's business.

The morning fragrance becomes more full throughout the day—a mowed alfalfa field, hay bales drying in the sun, dust from a walnut orchard's shaking, dairy cows moving toward the barn for their milking, the fermenting of the fruit that has been left on the tree or has fallen to the ground, too ripe to harvest, the beginning burns of fallen or thinned branches. These smells are somehow both celebratory and melancholy. They signal both the beginning and end.

When I was younger, the Valley's autumn fragrance meant school would begin again and I could be relieved of summer's doldrums. As I grow older, autumn signals so much more. I now understand the archetype of autumn: We finally celebrate our successes—the season's harvest, family, career, life — but as we are doing so, we realize that success often brings closure. Autumn's fragrance is full and powerful.

Take a drive through my Valley. Remember to roll the windows down.

ALICIA PAYNE SANDERSON

third-generation Valley native raising a fourth

William Keith (1838-1911)
Sunset near Suisun
watercolor on paper, 7-3/4 x 12 inches
The Oakland Museum of California:
The Wall Collection

Originally, the Cosumnes River Preserve was little more than a tree museum. In the 1980s, the Conservancy purchased eighty acres on the banks of the Cosumnes because they featured some trophy specimens of valley oak, considered the monarch of California oaks by virtue of their age, beauty, and size. But over the next few years, the Conservancy's vision for the Cosumnes evolved.

"Theoreticians would call what we practice here 'adaptive management,'" says Mike Eaton, director of the Cosumnes River project. "We try something, see if it works, and if it doesn't, we try something else."

One technique is tried and true—they buy land. Teaming with private organizations and government agencies, including Ducks Unlimited and the Bureau of Land Management, the Conservancy has purchased a number of farm properties, providing fields and marshland for the hundreds of thousands of migrating pintail, widgeon, snow geese, tundra swan, Canada geese, Ross's geese, phalaropes, grebes, sandpipers, egrets, and rails that migrate through the Central Valley. During Cali-

Granville
Redmond
(1871-1935)
California Oaks
oil on canvas,
22 x 36 inches
Private collection,
courtesy of
The Irvine Museum

fornia's economic downturn of the mid-1990s, the Conservancy was able to pluck the nearby 4,000-acre Valensin Ranch from a financially troubled developer who planned to build thousands of homes there. A family ranch since the days of the Mexican land grants, the Valensin property establishes a partial green belt between the expanding cities of Stockton and Sacramento. Walk the ranch today and you stroll across gently rolling grasslands never touched by a grader—a rarity in this part of the Central Valley—and pass vernal pools ringed in springtime with concentric circles of colorful wildflowers.

The Conservancy's formula for preserving the Cosumnes River ecosystem incorporates farming and ranching. For several years, the Conservancy has leased land at the Cosumnes Preserve to an organic rice grower. In 1999 the Preserve extended its embrace of agriculture by establishing a partnership with a privately-owned commercial farm. Jim and Sally Shanks manage the M & T Staten Ranch, a 9,000-acre farm on Staten Island in the Sacramento Delta. For years, the Shanks have farmed with a friendly eye toward wildlife. After harvesting their corn, wheat, and tomatoes, they flood land to provide habitat for migratory waterfowl. Each winter, 100,000 birds may visit Staten Island, including 18,000 sandhill cranes—believed to be the oldest avian species in the world. Now, with the guidance of Conservancy staff, the Shanks are restoring wetlands and riparian habitat. "It just seemed like a perfect fit for us to join up with the preserve," said Mrs. Shanks. "They're doing the same thing we are."

Upstream in the Sierra foothills, the Conservancy recently acquired a 12,000-acre chunk of the Howard Ranch, a verdant mixture of grasslands, blue oak woodlands, and spectacular vernal pools. After placing conservation easements on the land, the Conservancy plans to sell the property to a rancher who supports the idea of conscientious land stewardship.

The original core of the Cosumnes Preserve—those massive virgin oaks—are now witness to the happy marriage of environmental restoration and flood control. Many of the properties acquired for the preserve were once leveed farmlands. Working with the U.S. Army

Raymond Dabb Yelland (1848-1900)
Sunrise at Tracy, 1924
oil on canvas, 22 x 36 inches
The Oakland Museum of California: Gift of
Mr. and Mrs. William B. Land

Corps of Engineers, the Conservancy has removed or set back some of those levees. The Corps of Engineers terms this strategy "non-structural flood management." The idea is to give flooding rivers room to spread out, where they will not inflict serious damage. Shortly after the Cosumnes levees were removed in 1997, the river rose and flooded nearby fields. Waterfowl descended on the preserve, as did juvenile salmon. When the floods ebbed, thickets of willow and cottonwood began sprouting—natural reforestation at work.

Mike Eaton says, "To really see what we're doing here, you need a multi-generational perspective. Come back in a hundred years." In fact, you may not have to wait that long. Jeffrey Mount, a geology professor at the University of California at Davis, visited the Cosumnes shortly after the river shed its handcuffs. He declared, "Wildlife has exploded in response to a restored link between the floodplain and the river channel. Fish, insects, birds, mammals—all are using the flooded floodplain. There is a mellifluous roar of springtime life."

In many ways, the Cosumnes River Preserve embodies the efforts of The Nature Conservancy, not just in the Central Valley, but nation-wide. Once an organization dedicated to preserving endangered natural specimens, the Conservancy has come to understand that nature is not composed of isolated fragments. To save a piece, you have to save the entire puzzle. In the Central Valley, that means teaming with farmers, ranchers, fishermen, corporations, advocacy groups, and government agencies. Together, they are working to preserve the region's agricultural heritage, improve its flood safety, and restore the splendor of this bountiful landscape.

Thaddeus Welch
(1844-1919)
Jewett Ranch, 1893
oil on canvas,
29-3/4 x 49-3/4 inches
The Kern County Museum

THE SIERRA NEVADA

Changes in the Range of Light

"THE FOREST ABOUT US WAS DENSE AND COOL, THE SKY above us was cloudless and brilliant with sunshine. . . . Mountain domes, clothed with forests, scarred with landslides, cloven by canyons and valleys, and helmeted with glittering snow, fitly framed and finished the noble picture. . . . The eye was never tired of gazing, night or day, in calm or storm; it suffered but one grief, and that was that it could not look always, but must close sometimes in sleep." So Mark Twain described the Sierra Nevada in his 1872 classic *Roughing It*.

The Sierra Nevada enchants almost everyone—not just writers like Twain. Countless ordinary citizens consider this rugged landscape their special place, a land of quiet and solitude only a few hours from the grind of city life. While the Sierra is the preferred weekend getaway for millions, hundreds of thousands of Californians call it home. Between 1970 and 1990, the population of the Sierra Nevada doubled. Experts predict it will triple again over the next forty years.

John Muir, the bard of California's high country, suggested that the Sierra Nevada (Spanish for "snowy range") was misnamed and should have been called the "Range of Light." The great conservationist rejoiced in "the sunbursts of morning among the icy peaks, the noonday radiance on the trees and rocks and snow, the flush of the alpenglow, and a thousand dashing waterfalls with their marvelous abundance of irised spray." Look down and you might find a less lyrical source of all the luminosity. Most of the Sierra is built of highly reflective granite.

Ten to 15 million years ago, tectonic forces in what is now eastern California began thrusting up a gigantic mass of granite several hundred miles long and seventy-five miles wide—a batholith, in geologic

Hanson Puthuff
(1875-1972)
Mystical Hills
oil on canvas,
26 x 34 inches
The Irvine
Museum

terms. The Sierra batholith moved like a trapdoor hinged on its western edge. The uplift created a range of mountains with a steady elevation gain on the western slope and a precipitous drop to the east.

Climb most any peak in the Sierra Nevada, look around, and you will see a colossal meringue of cirques, ravines, cols, aretes, and minarets carved into granite by the action of ice and water. The Sierra Nevada includes more than 100 peaks over 13,000 feet high. Thirteen surpass 14,000 feet, including Mount Whitney. At 14,496 feet, Whitney is the tallest mountain in the United States outside Alaska.

In the Sierra Nevada, like most regions in California, a Mediterranean climate prevails. Summers are hot and dry, winters wet. As you climb in elevation, precipitation becomes more abundant and temperature swings more extreme. Mark Twain observed that in the Sierra "a lady who goes out visiting cannot hope to be prepared for all emergencies unless she takes her fan under one arm and her snowshoes under the other." Some higher slopes receive an average thirty feet of snow each year.

The Sierra Nevada harbors a tremendous diversity of wildlife. Although the Sierra constitutes less than twenty percent of California's land area, two-thirds of the state's bird and mammal species and over half the amphibian and reptile species can be found here. Scientists studying the Sierra have identified sixty-six different types of aquatic habitat, which support forty species of native fish. Eleven species are unique to the region, including the California golden trout, considered one of the most beautiful fish in the world. The Sierra Nevada also boasts at least 155 species of butterflies. In these mountains, you might see wolverine, Sierra bighorn sheep, California spotted owls, willow flycatchers, and limestone salamanders.

The flora of the Sierra Nevada is equally diverse. Over 3,500 plant species grow here, and of these, 400 are found nowhere else in the world. Throughout the higher altitudes of the Sierra, coniferous forests predominate, including vast stretches of Douglas fir, incense cedar, juniper, whitebark, Jeffrey, piñon, and Ponderosa pine. "The winds flow in melody through their colossal spires," wrote Muir about the trees of the Sierra, "and they are vocal everywhere with the songs of birds and running water." At the southern end of the Sierra grow the giant sequoia, the largest organisms on earth. When the first settlers began felling these astounding trees—a task that sometimes took several days per tree—they used the stumps for dance floors and Sunday schools. A twenty-six-foot-wide section of a sequoia was displayed at the Centennial Exhibition in Philadelphia in 1876. Easterners refused to believe it was part of a real tree.

The Sierra's Spine

The new moon smeared
with autumn clouds
I allow as harbingers
for a wet winter —
the Sierras between us again

& if I were truly romantic
I'd roach the mules
saddle an extra horse
ride three days
from Cedar Grove
& bring you home
the long way

instead I imagine
how this yellow crescent hangs
above the steep east wall
of granite and tailings

your mother
& two sisters camped
for the week
on Rock Creek
as you scatter
your father.

JOHN DOFFLEMYER, *rancher*
Reprinted with the permission of the author

William Keith (1838-1911)
Headwaters of the San Joaquin,
1878
oil on canvas, 40 x 72 inches
The Oakland Museum: Gift of
Elizabeth Keith Pond

Karl Yens (1868-1945)
Yosemite
oil on board, 24 x 18 inches
Private collection, courtesy of
The Irvine Museum

The U.S. Forest Service, the National Park Service, the Bureau of Land Management, and other public agencies together own seventy-six percent of the Sierra Nevada ecoregion. Within these public reserves lie some of America's most treasured landscapes, including a remarkable cluster of national parks, monuments, and wilderness areas in the central and southern Sierra. The imposing cliffs and towering waterfalls of Yosemite National Park inspire 4 million visitors each year. Kings Canyon National Park features a spectacular collection of mountains and alpine lakes, while Sequoia National Park and the recently designated Giant Sequoia National Monument shelter the largest remaining stands of giant sequoia.

Casual visitors who tour the famous parks and drive through seemingly endless forests might jump to the conclusion that the Sierra Nevada is a vast wilderness and will likely remain that way forever. While federal landholdings protect about ninety percent of the mountainous central and southern Sierra, development is booming in other parts of the range.

The Truckee, Walker, and Carson River valleys are feeling significant pressure, primarily due to rapid population growth in Reno and Carson City. Development is spreading from Truckee in Placer County all the way to Quincy in Plumas County, seventy-five miles to the north. Conservationists are especially concerned about the fate of the mountain valleys in this part of the northern Sierra. Only recently have scientists recognized the biological wealth of these unusual landscapes, still mostly owned by ranching families.

Sierra Valley, at 130,000 acres the largest montane valley in North America, encompasses the most extensive wetlands in the mountainous Sierra Nevada. Mountain wetlands are rare, and because of the widespread loss of wetlands in other parts of California, the marshes of Sierra Valley have gained particular significance. They help support the greatest abundance and diversity of bird life in the Sierra Nevada, attracting avian species from the Pacific Ocean, the Great Basin, and the Pacific flyway. During summer, long-billed curlews, Wilson's phalaropes, black-headed terns, snipe, shorebirds, ducks, geese, greater sandhill cranes, yellow-headed blackbirds, and white-faced ibis nest here. Fall brings large numbers of migratory raptors, such as Swainson's hawks, rough-legged hawks, prairie falcons, peregrine falcons, and bald eagles.

The rivers and lakes of the northern Sierra also hold biological treasure. In the Little Truckee River drainage, all seven of the original fish

Only in the High Places

THE AIR THINS, in what almost seems like a visual change of the atmosphere. A long, broad alluvial pitch climbs before us and hides our destination. Spewed out of the Lamarck Col in the distant past, this sloping ramp provides a cautioned invitation. As we hike higher, we feel the begrudging acceptance of these mountains deep in our lungs and legs. It is why we come: to feel alive in the most fundamental of ways. Only here, the east side of the Sierra Nevada, does the landscape provide us a perspective on ourselves and the basic functions of our planet.

The Sierra Nevada is really so many places in time and space. To understand it all, from the red cinder cones of the Owens Valley to the ghost pines of the western foothills, has always seemed overwhelming. The sheer magnitude of it all somehow seemed to drive me away, to send me to peaks and valleys of distant continents. But long days and cold nights in the Palisades made me realize the Sierra Nevada is my home mountain range. I go nowhere else when that unspeakable need for light, rock, and wind fills my being. Still, not all the parts of this spectacular mountain range are equal in their ability to draw me to the wind and rain. It is only the high places in which I focus my quest to know these mountains.

As we climb higher, Lamarck Col reveals itself in ways that only come with changes in elevation. As we leave the trail, car-size boulders lead us to a steep sun-cupped snowfield. My steps lighten and travel feels more natural as the terrain becomes a jumble of rocks and scree. Feet and hands on the rock make me understand, again, why we are here. The last steps to the top of the col are like the unwrapping of a gift. The Evolution Basin falls below my feet in a way that makes me feel like I might be able to fly. The pure and honest beauty of this moment leaves me with a physical joy. A warmth in the cold. A comfort in this harshness that provides us focus on all truth.

We find a sandy bench, and Darwin Canyon is ours alone. After we eat and drink, conversations become our measure of time. For some, this is a place best experienced alone. My past is filled with solitary days of whitebark pine and gritty Ramen noodles. Still, this night reminds me whom I love and how much more I love them here. We laugh in gasping, aching fits. We tell stories about the things most important to us. We argue. We talk of some things best forgotten but too momentous to leave behind.

The north face of Mount Darwin is in our near future. The excitement floats me just above sleep. Tomorrow's climb will give us another day in the high places. One more day to look down on the soaring ravens. One more day to feel the bite of winds shaped by this angular terrain. One more day to solve the many puzzles of long alpine routes. One more day to be followed by a lifetime of returns. The same places, the same people, the same indescribable joy of being.

ROBIN WILLS, *fire ecologist*

John Frost (1890-1937)
Near Lone Pine, California
oil on canvas, 30 x 36 inches
Private collection, courtesy of
The Irvine Museum

Edwin Deakin (1838-1923)
Donner Lake, From the Summit, 1876
oil on canvas, 44 x 72 inches
Courtesy of the Garzoli Gallery,
San Rafael

species survive, unlike many Sierra watersheds where human activity has decimated native fish. In nearby Independence Lake and its tributaries, a small number of Lahontan cutthroat trout cling to a precarious existence.

Lahontan cutthroat trout once swam in every tributary of the Truckee River between Lake Tahoe and Pyramid Lake in Nevada. (The Truckee River drains Lake Tahoe and empties into Pyramid Lake, a terminal alkaline desert lake in the Great Basin, north of Reno.) In the nineteenth century, Lahontan cutthroat trout sustained one of the most important freshwater fisheries in North America, rivaling the great salmon runs of the Central Valley rivers. Historically, these fish sometimes measured up to four feet and weighed up to sixty pounds. Fleets of fishing

boats sailed Pyramid Lake and Lake Tahoe in pursuit of this prized catch. The fishery crashed by 1928 due to dam building, erosion, logging mill effluents, and the introduction of exotic fish. Today, the original stock of Lahontan cutthroat trout survives in only a few isolated locations.

Over the last century, Lake Tahoe has experienced tremendous growth, but here, unlike in neighboring Reno, the tide of change may have already turned. The lake itself has always been renowned for its remarkable clarity. Describing a boat ride on Lake Tahoe, Mark Twain wrote, "So singularly clear was the water that when it was only twenty or thirty feet deep the bottom was so perfectly distinct that the boat seemed floating in the air!" Tahoe's water quality has been steadily

John Ross Key (1837-1920)
Lake Tahoe, 1870
oil on canvas, 15 x 30 inches
From the collection of Alfred Harrison,
courtesy of the North Point Gallery,
San Francisco

The Real California

LIKE SO MANY EASTERNERS and fortune-seekers before me, I crossed into California for the first time through a gap in the Sierra Nevada. I've never recovered from the sense of awe and fear those mountains inspire—would the old VW make it across?—or the delight of dropping down safe into the grassy foothills. The Pacific beckons, but for me the "real" California landscape is always rolling hills dotted with oaks, where towns are few and National Public Radio doesn't reach.

MARY D. NICHOLS
*Secretary for Resources,
State of California*

diminishing, mostly due to erosion caused by construction throughout the watershed. Today the Tahoe Conservancy, an independent state agency, works to protect open space in the Tahoe basin, and the Tahoe Regional Planning Authority limits real estate development. Their efforts and those of other organizations are aimed at preserving the lake's crystalline depths and saving much of Lake Tahoe's wild surroundings.

Unfortunately, the forecast may not be as bright for the Gold Country. Like the Truckee region to the east, the western foothills of the Sierra face heavy development pressure, due in large part to the proximity of Sacramento and the San Francisco Bay Area. Long-distance commuters are settling in the foothills, new businesses are establishing themselves, and retirees are flocking to the region. Working to protect the most precious natural resources from these trends, the Trust for Public Land and the American River Conservancy have acquired large parcels of private land along the American River and then transferred that land to the Bureau of Land Management and the Forest Service. These organizations are helping backpackers, fishermen, and river runners enjoy a wilderness experience along this beloved river, just as they have for decades. The American River Conservancy is also working to secure private lands throughout the headwaters of the Cosumnes, and

Charles Dormon Robinson
(1847-1933)
Crest of the Sierra, 1909
oil on canvas, 42 x 81 inches
Crocker Art Museum, Sacramento:
Gift of Miss Lillian M. Robinson,
Conserved with funds donated by
Alfred Harrison,
North Point Gallery, San Francisco

Benjamin Brown
(1865-1942)
Autumn Glory
oil on canvas,
28 x 36 inches
The Irvine
Museum

its efforts complement those of The Nature Conservancy downstream at the Cosumnes River Preserve (see page 76).

Urbanization has not fully advanced into the southwestern foothills of the Sierra, but with the cities of the Central Valley growing rapidly, experts predict that this region too will eventually experience the same growing pains felt by other parts of the Sierra. In the foothills along the South Fork of the Kern River grows a large riparian forest of cottonwood and willow. A bird-watchers' paradise, these woods attract up to 240 different species. Set up your scope and you might spot willow flycatchers, tricolored blackbirds, and white-throated swifts. The site is equally exciting for butterfly enthusiasts. Sixty percent of California's butterfly species can be found within a few miles of the Kern River Preserve. One species, the Eunus skipper, was believed extinct until it was recently rediscovered here.

In the 1980s, representatives of the National Audubon Society brought the natural wealth of the Kern River area to the attention of The Nature Conservancy. The Conservancy responded by establishing the Kern River Preserve. Since then, hundreds of volunteers have helped replant the riparian forest. The number of nesting pairs of endangered yellow-billed cuckoos and other rare songbirds has increased, indicative of improving health for this riparian ecosystem. With restoration efforts well under way, the Conservancy handed

The "Oasis of the Sierras"

IN 1870, MARK HOPKINS, THE RECLUSIVE CO-FOUNDER OF THE
Central Pacific Railroad, sought the advice of a Native American as to where he might find the most beautiful place in
the Sierra Nevada mountains to build a cabin for himself
and his wife, Mary. He was led on a four-hour ride along a
crude road, winding from the Donner Summit area into the
headwaters of the North Fork of the American River, where
natural carbonic springs rise from the ground all about.

"Our people call this place 'The Oasis of the Sierras,'" Hopkins's guide told him, as they stood by a waterfall
overlooking a wildflower-filled meadow at the base of the
Sierra crest below Anderson Peak and Tinker's Knob. Hopkins proceeded to build his four-room log cabin there, as
well as the Old Soda Springs Hotel, to bring guests into the
valley so that his wife would not become lonely. The hotel
operated from 1873 to 1898, when it burned down from a
guest's kerosene lamp.

Hopkins's family sold the property in 1914 to Josiah
Stanford (Leland Stanford's nephew), and he in turn sold it
to my grandfather, Allen L. Chickering, in 1928. Remaining
from the days of the hotel are Hopkins's cabin (1875), Tim-
othy Hopkins's lodge (1899), a barn, and several other
cabins from the last century. Here I am privileged to spend
five months a year, ten miles from the nearest store (at
Soda Springs, named after the springs in our meadow),
amidst wildflowers, a rushing river, 9,000-foot peaks, and
the largest example of Indian petroglyphs in the entire
Sierra Nevada range.

Our family donated conservation easements on 1,800
acres in 1974 to the University of California, motivated by
my grandfather's (Allen's) and my father's (Sherman's) avid
interest in botany and wildness: They spent their latter years
studying and cataloguing the numerous species of wildflowers on this land. Today,
this valley is preserved forever—still, and always, "The Oasis of the Sierras."

NICHOLAS R. CHICKERING, *sixth-generation Californian*

William F. Jackson (1850-1936)
Poppies and Trees - American River Bluffs
oil on canvas, 12 x 18 inches
The Redfern Gallery, Laguna Beach

over management of the Kern River Preserve to the Audubon Society in 1998.

When pondering the environmental future of the Sierra Nevada, you cannot ignore the activities of the U.S. Forest Service, which owns more than half of this mountainous terrain. For decades, logging, mining, and ranching were the economic mainstays of the high country, but tourism has eclipsed their value, as has the cumulative influx of new residents drawn to the region for its aesthetic appeal. The Forest Service has made halting efforts to balance timber and mining interests with the public's increasing concern for environmental protection. It has declared areas to be roadless, conducted comprehensive studies, and facilitated cooperation among the seven National Forests in the Sierra.

In recent years, the Quincy Library Group, an outspoken coalition of loggers and environmentalists, has pressured the Forest Service to alter their management practices in ways that might increase timber harvests but also protect sensitive habitat and minimize the impact of wildfires. Over the last century, human activity has disrupted natural wildfire patterns in the high country, and now catastrophic wildfires sometimes erupt. Some scientists believe that fire represents the most pressing threat to biodiversity in the forests of the Sierra Nevada.

The controversy sparked by the Quincy Library Group may be symptomatic of a larger problem. According to Ed Hastey, former California Director of the U.S. Bureau of Land Management, the Forest Service "needs to be thinking on a sub-regional basis, developing a multi-species, multi-habitat approach." Planning should include private lands, particularly in areas where development poses the biggest threat to the natural integrity of the Sierra Nevada. Hastey points to the efforts of San Diego County as a model for large-scale environmental planning (see page 30).

Placer County, the fastest-growing county in the state, is thinking along those lines. Officials there are developing a planning process that promotes business growth, allows for housing development, but also maintains the county's natural heritage. Essentially, they are embracing concepts put forth by another local organization, the Sierra Business Council. Founded in 1994, the Sierra Business Council is a coalition of 500 member organizations, mostly business interests, that believe the region's most critical economic asset is its scenic beauty. The Council is working with communities to promote

William Keith
Upper Kern River, 1876
75-1/8 x 123-1/4 inches
Iris & B. Gerald Cantor Center for
Visual Arts at Stanford University:
Stanford Family Collections

forms of economic growth that do not squander the Sierra Nevada's
natural wealth.

Although much of the Sierra Nevada is under public stewardship,
that status alone may not stave off future environmental problems. The
Nature Conservancy has identified the northern Sierra mountains and
the southern Sierra foothills as two regions of outstanding biological
diversity that face imminent threats. Currently, the Conservancy is
launching projects to protect natural communities in both areas. Many
other local and national organizations are also working in the Sierra
Nevada to secure its environmental future. Fortunately, there is still time
to ensure that the Range of Light, John Muir's "most divinely beautiful
of all mountain chains," will remain a place all Californians treasure.

Lorenzo Latimer (1857-1941)
*Keiths Dome from Middle Trail to
Mount Tallac*, 1917
watercolor on paper,
10-1/2 x 13-1/2 inches
From the collection of Bill Landreth,
courtesy of the North Point Gallery,
San Francisco

SHASTA-CASCADES

A Landscape Intact

WHILE MUCH OF CALIFORNIA SUFFERS FROM PROBLEMS OF overcrowding and overdevelopment, the Shasta-Cascades region confronts the opposite set of concerns. Sparsely populated, the Shasta-Cascades and the adjacent Modoc Plateau are sometimes called California's "Empty Quarter." Here in northeastern California, the most pressing regional worries are a slow-growing economy and the decline of extractive industries like mining and logging. Yet an irony of conservation is that a languishing economy can be a good tonic for the land. Certainly, the Shasta-Cascades can boast one of the most unspoiled natural environments in California.

The Shasta-Cascades, as they are loosely defined in this chapter, stretch from the Klamath Mountains in Siskiyou County north to the Oregon border, east to Nevada, and south to Lassen County, where the Cascade Range and the Sierra Nevada intersect. The Cascades are considered ecologically distinct from the Sierra because of their different geologic origin. The Sierra Nevada is mostly granite while the Cascade Range is volcanic, as is the neighboring Modoc Plateau in the extreme northeastern corner of the state.

Although the terrain of the Modoc Plateau, a dry tableland blanketed with sagebrush scrub and juniper woodlands, strikes many observers as monotonously flat, in fact it is crisscrossed by jagged volcanic trenches. This fissured landscape set the scene for California's one major Indian conflict, which escalated to warlike proportions because of the region's topography. In 1872, several bands of the Modoc tribe, led by a charismatic leader named Captain Jack, staged a five-month-long guerilla war from the Modoc Plateau's labyrinth of volcanic trenches. Although they numbered only sixty fighting men, the Modocs

Thomas Hill (1829-1908)
Indian Camp, Mt. Shasta,
California, 1893
oil on canvas, 36 x 59 inches
Courtesy of the Garzoli Gallery,
San Rafael

The Klamath Basin

William Keith (1838-1911)
Klamath Lake with Pelicans and Mount McLaughlin, c. 1908
oil on canvas, 22 x 32 inches
Collection of the Hearst Art Gallery,
St. Mary's College of
California: Gift of
Averell Harriman, 1948

TREMENDOUS STRETCHES OF FOREST sloping off the flanks of snow-capped mountains to a sea of sagebrush; expansive marshes teeming with wildlife; blue-ribbon trout streams meandering through large cattle ranches; all under a big sky that dominates the landscape.

Scenes such as these conjure thoughts of Montana, Wyoming, Idaho, or eastern Oregon. In reality, these descriptions of the land come from my experiences in the northeastern corner of California, called the Modoc Plateau by some. I favor that portion known as the Klamath Basin. In particular, it is the wetlands, with their variety and abundance of bird life, that draw me.

The noted wildlife painter Francis Lee Jacques (1887-1969) was excited almost exclusively by the presence of larger birds. Once, when his wife complained that she couldn't see warblers quickly enough to name them, he made his often-quoted remark, "Never mind, the difference between warblers and no warblers is very slight." I think Jacques and I would have been kindred spirits, for as a professional wildlife photographer and naturalist, I find great joy in the wide sky of the Klamath Basin and the big birds it holds.

In winter months, hundreds of eagles, both golden and bald, can be seen daily leaving their night roosts in the stands of old growth timber on the surrounding mountains. Flying out to spend the day on frozen marshes, eating the dead and dying waterfowl that succumb to the deep, deep cold that cloaks the Klamath Basin, this is the largest wintering concentration of bald eagles in the continental United States. Some eagles are known to come from as far away as the Northwest Territories in Canada.

Springtime finds the skies filled with northward-migrating ducks and geese that stop over in the Klamath Basin to gain weight for their continued flight to the Canadian prairies and the Arctic. Seeing long, white lines of snow geese beating into a strong spring wind against a storm-black sky, I am reminded of so many strings of pearls.

The blood-red dawn of summer finds sandhill cranes silhouetted in the sky, moving back and forth from feeding areas to nest sites as they have done for thousands of years. By midday during these dog days of summer, white pelicans spiral upward in thermals, looking like the great white-sailed ships of days of old. These birds have left the tules far below and are one of the last-remaining breeding colonies in California.

For me, it all comes together in the fall. Viewing the tremendous flocks of ducks and geese from the Siberian, Alaskan, and Canadian Arctic as they drop out of a sky laced with clouds from Mexican storms into a marsh on the Klamath Basin, I truly see the woven bond of our hemisphere and the role of the landscape in saving our wildlife and in inspiring mankind.

F.L. Jacques would have loved the Klamath Basin in the fall. For instead of the singular warbler, the Klamath Basin holds the largest concentration of waterfowl in North America, and possibly the world. More animal hearts than human hearts beat here. It is my favorite landscape in California.

TUPPER ANSEL BLAKE
wildlife photographer and naturalist

knew the land intimately and they used it to their fullest advantage, turning it into a bewildering deathtrap for the U.S. Army until reinforced federal troops ultimately overwhelmed the Modocs.

At the northwestern edge of the Modoc Plateau is another historic site—albeit a less bloody one. The Lower Klamath Basin is home to one of the nation's first waterfowl refuges, set aside by Theodore Roosevelt in 1908. Every autumn the lakes, marshes, and farmlands of the Klamath Basin host a wildlife spectacular. Millions of geese, ducks, and other waterfowl descend on this area during their annual migration from summer ranges as far away as Siberia. Flocks of pintails, widgeon, and snow geese nearly blacken the sky. During warmer months the region is

Juan B. Wandesford (1817-1902)
Devil's Castle, Trinity Alps, c. 1867
oil on canvas, 20 x 30 inches
From the collection of Drs. Charles and Caroline Scielzo, courtesy of the North Point Gallery, San Francisco

also a center of bird life, providing breeding grounds for American white pelicans, grebes, cinnamon teal, and greater sandhill crane.

To the west of the Cascades rise the Klamath Mountains, heavily forested and thinly settled, a complex assemblage of mountains including the Siskiyou, Salmon, and Trinity Ranges. The Klamath Mountains support the greatest variety of coniferous trees in North America. Botanists believe that over millennia, coniferous tree species from the Sierra Nevada, Cascade, and Coast Ranges expanded their ranges to include this area. Moist summers and mild winters have allowed these trees to survive here, along with madrone, tan oak, canyon live oak, orchids, and so much azalea that writer David Rains Wallace describes a Klamath forest as smelling like "a roomful of fancy women."

Two great volcanoes, Lassen Peak and Mount Shasta, dominate the southern end of the Cascade Range. The snowy cone of Mount Shasta rises to 14,162 feet, the sixth-highest peak in California. Unlike California's other great mountains, Shasta stands alone, 10,000 feet higher than the surrounding countryside. The poet Joaquin Miller wrote, "Lonely as God, and white as a winter moon, Mount Shasta starts up sudden and solitary from the heart of the great black forests of Northern California." For decades, Shasta's remote and brooding presence has fascinated metaphysical cults of many stripes. One group claims that gnomes live on Shasta in caves of gold. Another proclaims Shasta to be the home of the Lemurians, a lost race that fled their Eden-like home on the continent of Mu before it sank into the Pacific. A 1930s book espousing that belief sent thousands of seekers into the surrounding national forest, beating the bushes in hopes of discovering paradise on the flanks of a dormant volcano.

William Keith (1838-1911)
Mount Shasta and McCloud River
oil on canvas, 36 x 59 inches
Collection of the Hearst Art Gallery,
St. Mary's College of California: Gift of
F.C. Dougherty, 1955

A year-round snowcap tops the ethereal Mount Shasta, and runoff feeds the Shasta, Sacramento, and McCloud Rivers. The icy waters and pristine forest of the McCloud River Valley make it one of the premier fishing streams in the nation, even though Shasta Dam, erected downstream on the Sacramento in 1944, put an end to the McCloud's great salmon and steelhead trout runs. In 1973, the McCloud Fishing Club donated a 2,330-acre portion of their landholdings along the McCloud River to The Nature Conservancy. After studying this property, the Conservancy determined it could sustain limited fishing. At the McCloud River Preserve, only ten anglers at a time can drop their lines into a three-mile stretch of river. Hooks must be barbless, and the creel limit is zero. All fishing is catch and release, but if you're lucky, you might land a wild Shasta Rainbow trout.

From Washington State to California, volcanic peaks like Mount Shasta dot the Cascade Range. Before Mount Saint Helens erupted in 1980, Lassen Peak, southernmost of the Cascade summits, had the distinction of the being the most recently active volcano in the continental United States In 1914, Lassen began a series of small eruptions that lasted a year until 1915, when the mountain blew its top in a huge explosion, spewing ash seven miles into the sky. Molten lava melted Lassen's snowpack, triggering an eighteen-mile-long mudslide. The volcano continued to erupt intermittently until 1921, when it returned to its slumbers.

Today the foothills of Lassen Peak are characterized by rolling grasslands, oak woodlands, and basalt-capped mesas. The largest migratory deer herd in California winters on the Lassen foothills, then travels to the high country during summer. Many crystal-clear streams slice through the foothills, and they support a rich diversity of songbirds, including yellow warbler and common yellowthroat, both of which have declined in more developed areas. The Lassen foothills are the land of Ishi, America's "last wild Indian," as he is sometimes called. In 1911, Ishi, generally believed to be the sole surviving member of the Yahi tribe, emerged after years of hiding in the Lassen foothills.

The Lassen foothills have changed little since Ishi's day, largely because the land is held by relatively few owners, mostly large ranches and state and federal agencies. Some families have raised cattle on the Lassen foothills for five generations. In this region, ranching has often proven harmonious with the surrounding healthy ecosystems, providing habitat not just for cattle but a wide array of native plants and animals.

Unfortunately, change is looming. To the west, the Central Valley cities of Redding and Chico are expanding. The spread of suburban housing into the Lassen foothills threatens to slice up this largely intact 800,000-acre ecosystem. The Lassen foothills are home to some of the largest unfragmented blue oak woodlands in the state. Named for the hue of its leaves during late summer, blue oak is unique to California, yet throughout the state almost no significant stands of this lovely tree are protected within government reserves. Also at risk in the Lassen foothills are rare native wildflowers and small seasonal ponds called vernal pools. Once common throughout the Central Valley, vernal pools constitute one of California's most threatened landscapes.

For years, The Nature Conservancy has maintained preserves in the lower elevations of the Lassen foothills, but in 1999, the Conservancy took a giant step toward safeguarding the region's natural heritage by purchasing a conservation easement on the 36,000-acre Denny Ranch, an area bigger than the City of San Francisco. The largest conservation easement in California history, this landmark agreement will keep the property functioning as a privately owned cattle ranch while

Thomas Hill (1829-1908)
Mill Creek Canyon
oil on canvas, 48-3/4 x 84-1/4 inches
Crocker Art Museum,
Sacramento:
Bequest of Anna C. Brommero

A Wilderness Legacy

I GREW UP IN THE WILDERNESS—in the sense that, whenever they could, my parents would take us camping as deep into the desert or Sierra as we could get. My grandfather was a great friend of John Muir's, and my mother used to tell us stories of camping with them in the Sierra in the early 1900s, when she was just a child. Muir never got lost in the mountains, she said, but when he visited her family in Washington, D.C., he would invariably lose his way within blocks of their home!

Because of their own love of the wild, my parents tried to plant early the knowledge that wilderness areas and open space are beyond precious, and that for us all, they are an irreplaceable and essential source of genuine joy, strength, renewal, and peace of mind. As an artist, I hope to give back to these lands a little of what they have given me, by attempting to capture on canvas some of what it is that makes us all so passionate about preserving these remaining treasures of California.

The experiences that the wild has given our family have often been magical; all have been memorable; and all are permanently engraved in my memory:

sitting still for hours so that a beaver can continue cutting down an aspen undisturbed; getting drenched to the skin when the tent collapses after an all-night downpour, and laughing at our sodden state; watching an osprey dive for a trout, flip his dinner in mid-air and circle the lake with it for a long time before devouring it on a nearby branch; thrilling at the sight of a mountain lion launching himself over the trail from a ledge in front of us and disappearing soundlessly into the forest; or wriggling on our elbows, in a most ungraceful way, across a wet high country meadow so as not to let the golden trout see us coming, and then, still on our stomachs, casting our flies out into the stream for our dinner; watching crimson sunsets from our camp, in the desert or at 10,000 feet, and later marveling at the stars. How lucky we've been to live in California.

ZENAIDA MOTT, *founding member, Baywood Artists*

preventing future subdivision. The Nature Conservancy hopes to acquire conservation easements on other properties throughout the region, piecing together a mosaic of protected private property and public land that together constitute a biologically intact working landscape. Peggy McNutt, director of the Lassen Foothills Project, says, "Five years ago some ranchers would have never talked to me. But we all see what's been lost in other areas, and now we're at the table."

Another goal of the Lassen Foothills Project is to restore the landscape to its full vigor. Teaming with local ranchers, Conservancy staff members conduct prescribed burns to control exotic weeds. In some areas, stewards are experimenting with techniques to resurrect native grasslands. Recently, they have had success with a method developed in Australia. Seed plants are cut and baled like hay, then spread across the property being revegetated.

Five major streams descend from the Lassen foothills and flow into the Sacramento River. Four connect the Lassen Foothills Project with lands targeted by The Nature Conservancy's Sacramento River Project (see page 73). Although all of these streams support steelhead trout and salmon, the most notable is Battle Creek. Before it was dammed fifty years ago, the deep, shaded gorges of Battle Creek functioned as one of the most important spawning grounds in the Sacramento Valley, hosting all four runs of Chinook salmon—winter, fall, late-fall, and spring. Chinook are named for the time of year when adult fish pass through the Golden Gate on their way toward spawning grounds.

Battle Creek is fed by underground springs, so its waters remain cool year round. Most streams and rivers that drain into the Central Valley are fed by mountain runoff. Their water temperatures rise as flows diminish during summer and fall. Winter-run Chinook spawn in the summer, and spring-run Chinook spawn in the fall. The adult fish and the eggs they lay require cold temperatures to survive. Battle Creek is the only tributary of the Sacramento below Shasta Dam with water chilly enough to sustain winter-run Chinook, now classified as an endangered species.

Recognizing the significance of Battle Creek, The Nature Conservancy has been working to restore its native salmon runs. Pacific Gas and Electric owns eight dams on Battle Creek. For two years, the Conservancy met with Pacific Gas and Electric, the California Department of Fish and Game, the Battle Creek Watershed Conservancy, the U.S. Bureau of Reclamation, the U.S. Fish and Wildlife Service, the National Marine Fisheries Service, and many other public and private organizations. Those discussions resulted in a plan to restore forty-two miles of salmon run on Battle Creek by removing five dams, improving fish screens and ladders on the remaining three, and adjusting the release of water from those dams to match natural, seasonal flows.

Nearby on Butte Creek, four small dams were recently taken out, and the salmon population has exploded. Fishery advocates believe the same could happen on Battle Creek. Don Koch, California Department of Fish and Game regional manager in Redding, says the Battle Creek restoration "is truly a gift from the past." Adds Peggy McNutt, "The Battle Creek effort was unique. A group of private individuals and public organizations looked beyond the standard conflicts and found a way to crack open a solution. I was proud to be involved."

Throughout much of California, The Nature Conservancy struggles to piece together fragments of the natural habitat insto something resembling whole cloth. In the Lassen foothills, a different opportunity awaits. Here the Conservancy has a chance to secure an entire ecosystem while it is still intact. By preserving a working environment like the Lassen foothills, The Nature Conservancy is saving livelihoods as well as land. Similar opportunities await throughout the untrammeled Shasta-Cascades.

THE NORTH COAST
Saving the California Dream

CALIFORNIA'S NORTH COAST IS A LAND OF EMERALD FORESTS and rugged, boulder-strewn shorelines. Here, the bark of a sea lion on a misty morning or the hushed silence of a redwood forest are common-place experiences. Indeed, few places in the United States are blessed with such natural beauty. The North Coast seems to epitomize California's remarkable natural endowment. Yet, the region stretching from Sonoma County in the south to Del Norte on the Oregon border confronts pressing environmental concerns. Most stem from the region's principal economic activity: logging.

Lining the full length of the North Coast is the rugged Coast Range, mostly blanketed with lush coniferous forests. Short, swift rivers like the Mattole, Mad, and Smith rivers race down steep valleys carved into the mountains. The Smith is the only complete river system in California that flows to the sea uninterrupted by a dam. In southern Humboldt County, the King Range, a spur of the Coast Range, abruptly rises 4,000 feet above the sea. This steep mountain chain presents such a formidable barrier that all major highways swing inland to avoid it. The result is the Lost Coast, a fifty-mile stretch of isolated shoreline wilderness charac-terized by jagged cliffs, sea stacks, black sand beaches, waterfalls, and rain—lots of rain. Throughout the North Coast, the climate is cool and foggy in the summer, rainy in the winter. At higher elevations, snow is common. Parts of the North Coast receive 100 inches of rain annually, but that's just an average. Some years are really wet. Because of the heavy precipitation, North Coast vegetation approaches conditions resembling a temperate rain forest. Rhododendrons run riot. Ferns grow ten feet high. A tremendous variety of mushrooms flourishes.

Travel north along the coast from San Francisco and you will almost certainly be struck by the untouched nature of the shoreline.

Carl Von Perbandt
(1832-1911)
Pomo Indians
Camped at
Fort Ross, 1886
oil on canvas
mounted on
masonite,
54 x 84 inches
The Oakland
Museum of
California
Kahn Collection

William Keith (1838-1911)
Twilight at Cazadero, 1910-1911
oil on canvas, 22 x 28 inches
Collection of the Hearst Art Gallery,
Saint Mary's College of California:
Gift of L L. Lindley
Scott McCue Photography

You can drive all the way to Oregon and, except for a few towns, pass only scattered, unobtrusive housing. Only one Californian in a hundred calls the North Coast home. Certainly, the sparse population and remote location help maintain the integrity of the oceanfront here, but many organizations have worked to maintain the precious natural resources of the North Coast. Perhaps the most notable are two state agencies: the California Coastal Commission and the California Coastal Conservancy.

The Coastal Commission, established by voter initiative in 1972, regulates development in the coastal zone, which generally extends 1,000 yards inland from the sea. Since its inception, the Coastal Commission has been dogged by controversy. Environmentalists complain it approves almost all the projects it reviews. Homeowners and developers charge the commission with abusing private property rights and issuing unreasonable and arbitrary requirements. The commission has endured brushes with corruption, staff cuts, and endless political bickering. Nonetheless, the shoreline of the North Coast—as well as much of the Central Coast—remains a spectacular and relatively untrammeled place. The hurdles that the Coastal Commission places before builders have helped forestall the shoulder-to-shoulder development that blights so many other coastal regions of the United States.

Working alongside the Coastal Commission is the California Coastal Conservancy, chartered by the state legislature to restore, protect, and maintain public access to the state's 1,100-mile shoreline.

Raymond Dabb Yelland (1848-1900)

Mendocino Coast

oil on canvas, 28-1/2 x 44-1/2 inches

Courtesy of the Garzoli Gallery, San Rafael

Gottardo Piazzoni (1872-1945)
Gualala Bay, Northern Tip of Sonoma Coast, 1904
oil on board, 10-3/4 x 13-1/4 inches
From the collection of Barbara and Michael Janeff, courtesy of the North Point Gallery, San Francisco

Since its founding in 1976, the Coastal Conservancy has helped preserve more than 35,000 acres of wetlands, dunes, wildlife habitat, and farmland, and has opened miles of coastline to public use. The Coastal Conservancy has engaged in hundreds of projects up and down the state. Recently, the Coastal Conservancy teamed with the Trust for Public Land to obtain 3,900 acres in the Lost Coast region. They conveyed the property to a coalition of eleven Native American tribes, who manage and restore the property, demonstrating how tribal traditions work in harmony with nature. Among their many other projects, the Coastal Conservancy is developing management plans for the Russian River in Sonoma County, protecting coastline near Fort Bragg, and preserving and restoring marshes in Humboldt and Del Norte counties.

Besides the North Coast's wild seashore, the other predominant natural feature here is forest. Vast wooded tracts, mostly Douglas fir and redwood, clothe the hills. The region boasts one of the most impressive concentrations of big trees on the planet. Anyone who has ever ventured into a grove of virgin redwoods remembers the experience—trunks ten feet to fifteen feet across, crowns reaching incredible heights, some taller than the Statue of Liberty. In 1863, William H. Brewer wrote, "They grow so abundant that the sun cannot penetrate through the dense and deep mass of foliage overhead. A damp shady atmosphere pervades the forests, and luxuriant ferns and thick underwood often clothe the ground. Large trees fall, mosses and ferns grow over the prostrate trunks, trees spring up among them on the thick

Julian Rix (1850-1903)
Twilight Scene with Stream and Redwood Trees
oil on canvas, 83-1/2 x 46-1/2 inches
The Oakland Museum of California:
Bequest of Dr. Cecil E. Nixon

decaying wood. . . . A deep silence reigns. . . ." Redwoods grow in what might be called California's fog belt, at altitudes below 3,000 feet, in a region 450 miles long and no more than thirty-five miles from the coast. Despite these geographic limitations, virgin redwood forests once covered nearly 2 million acres from southern Oregon to Big Sur. Less than three percent of those forests survive today.

Several state parks and Redwoods National Park have secured most existing remnants of old-growth redwoods, but until recently, the last significant privately-owned stand grew in the upper reaches of two Humboldt County streams, an area that became known as the Headwaters Forest. A vitriolic battle to save the Headwaters pitted a band of local environmentalists against the Pacific Lumber Company and its financier owners. In 1996, after years of protests and posturing from both sides, the state and federal governments struck a deal with Pacific Lumber to preserve over 5,000 acres of old-growth redwoods in the Headwaters, along with some surrounding buffer zones. The government paid a per-acre price more in line with suburban development than timber harvesting. Despite that agreement, disputes continue, with environmentalists pressing their concerns for species like the marbled murrelet, a seabird that nests exclusively in old-growth forest, and the coho and Chinook salmon.

The fate of the region's salmon fisheries may be the next major conflict to rack the North Coast. Once this region was renowned for its anadromous fish—species that live most of their lives in the sea but swim up rivers to spawn. In the nineteenth century the waterways of the North Coast boiled with migrating Chinook salmon, some of them behemoths weighing up to 100 pounds. The sight of a salmon run was enough to spook horses. People used pitchforks to scoop fish from rivers. In the 1880s, Richard Hume, who amassed a fortune in the Pacific Northwest

canning salmon, wrote of the Klamath River, "I had never seen so many [salmon] in such a small stream in my life." But as early as the 1890s, North Coast salmon runs began to decline. In recent decades, Chinook populations have plunged, along with coho salmon and steelhead trout.

Many experts blame logging. When a forest is razed, erosion occurs, filling potential spawning grounds with sediment. Shallower water and the loss of shade from surrounding trees results in higher water temperatures. Salmon require cold water to survive. The logging community counters that salmon have been over-fished on land and at sea and that natural variations in weather, particularly some extended droughts, have suppressed salmon populations. Currently, several North Coast counties are cooperating with state and federal officials to develop a coordinated strategy for saving the salmon fisheries, an effort that includes restoring watersheds, evaluating road management techniques, and developing fish-friendly land-use practices.

One sure way to save streams and forest is to buy them. For decades, a few organizations have been doing just that along the North Coast. In the 1920s, the Save the Redwoods League began acquiring redwood forest land and turning it over for inclusion in a state or national park. More recently, the Trust for Public Land has also been actively acquiring land along the North Coast. The Nature Conservancy, too, can take credit for preserving a substantial piece of the region's primeval forest.

In 1907, businessman Heath Angelo traveled by logging train and stagecoach into the Coast Range of northern California. He found a land of clear streams and rugged mountains blanketed by virgin stands of redwood and Douglas fir. Angelo fell in love with the country and returned often. In 1931, he and his wife Marjorie bought a homestead on Elder Creek, a tributary of the South Fork of the Eel River. The Men-

docino County property was home to mink, deer, bear, fox, bobcats, and river otter. Over the years, the Angelos acquired more land until they owned 3,000 acres of old-growth Douglas fir, redwood, and deciduous trees.

In 1959, the Angelos sold their property—at a fraction of its market value—to The Nature Conservancy. It was the Conservancy's first acquisition in the western United States. The Angelos' wish was that their property function as an educational resource. One of the largest undisturbed watersheds in northern California, the property provides a valuable research tool for studying salmon and steelhead spawning and observing the habits of rare creatures like red-backed voles, Olympic salamanders, and the poster child of environmental conflict, the northern spotted owl.

The Nature Conservancy managed the Angelos' land until 1994, when it transferred ownership of what is now called the Angelo Coast Range Preserve to the University of California's Natural Reserve System, the largest collection of university-operated natural reserves in the world. The Angelo Preserve, in conjunction with 3,500 adjoining acres owned by the Bureau of Land Management, continues to serve as a biological treasure trove for researchers and a place of inspiration for ordinary citizens.

Along the North Coast, the Nature Conservancy has also been active in other projects. Near Eureka, the Conservancy has worked to protect what many consider the most pristine coastal dunes in the Pacific Northwest. In the 1940s, William M. and Hortense M. Lanphere, biologists at Humboldt State College, purchased property at the northern end of the Samoa Peninsula, which encloses Arcata Bay. The Lanpheres had a fondness for places where "coyotes howl and the wind blows free," according to Hortense Lanphere. The young biologists

The Eel Endures

THE EEL RIVER WAS NAMED FOR FISH. Early European explorers saw Native Americans carrying lampreys, swapped them a busted skillet for the fresh catch, and memorialized their meal with a name. And so, on one of California's three dozen major stream systems, a river's actual denizens were honored, instead of explorers (as on the Smith River) or the iconography of new settlers (Merced, Sacramento, San Joaquin, American).

The Eel writhes like a four-pronged stroke of lightning across the Northern California landscape. It falls from fir, pine, and hardwood-clad peaks of the Coast Range, shoots north through dense, cool redwood groves, and runs to sea through a broad, fertile delta south of Eureka.

Paint it by numbers. The Eel drains 3,600 square miles of Mendocino, Humboldt, Trinity, and Lake counties, and annually flows with more than 6 million acre-feet of turbid water. Running past friable Franciscan Formation soils, it also totes a huge burden of erosion, more than any other river except China's Yellow (Huang Ho). One hundred million tons of sediment gouted downstream in the great flood of 1964, when an awesome flow of 752,000 cubic feet per second was recorded at Scotia—ten times the ordinary peak flow of the Colorado.

Some of its major flows have faded to a trickle. Thirty years ago, 100,000 spawning steelhead and 90,000 silver and king salmon swam in from the sea to call it home. Now endangered species status is invoked for the silvers and steelies, and kings are paupers in their former realm.

Paint it by memories. Drinking from a cold feeder creek of the Middle Fork Eel in the Yolla Bolly Wilderness. Swimming in a pool full of summer steelhead at a spot downstream. Barely escaping from a whitewater raft wrapped around a rock in the dangerous rapid called Coal Mine. Raptly watching steelhead spawn in shallows of the upper Main Stem on an icy day. Then, in spring, launching a sea kayak below Van Arsdale dam and paddling 150 miles to the sea in five days.

Hiking among the lush mosses and ancient yews of Elder Creek on the upper South Fork, a place so pristine its waters establish a benchmark of purity. Then, kayaking the Branscomb Run downstream during high water after a winter storm, getting trapped in the recirculating hole of a rapid, and feeling the muscles of one shoulder start to shred while my boat lurched and trembled in the grip of the tumbling water's fury.

And that calm day when my rod bent into a crescent and its reel screamed as a wild steelhead snatched my lure, then swiftly and contemptuously spat it out. He prevented me from the full rubric of catch-and-release, yet left me transfigured with happiness. A kiss of raw, native energy, of savage freedom and relentless purpose, had been tattooed upon my soul.

Nowadays, the Eel has been plundered, many of its forests mowed, its crumbling banks and slopes denuded. However, a giant heist has been fended off. Once the Eel was to be diverted, its waters exported to further the wealth of Central Valley corporate farms. Saved from that fate, it still flows. Parks and preserves still hold segments of the watershed's old lands and old ways. And some people seek to stabilize slopes, rebuild spawning areas, and replant native vegetation.

A millennium from now, Californians may count restoration of the Eel's health as one of their major achievements. Shocked by aqueous lightning, a man may so dream.

PAUL McHUGH, *journalist*

Thomas Hill (1829-1908)
View of Scotia Bluffs
oil on board, 11-1/2 x 17 inches.
Crocker Art Museum, Sacramento
Gift of Dr. Hertzl Friedlander

Trinidad Coast, California

Jack Wilkinson Smith (1873-1949)
Fog-Veiled Coast
oil on canvas, 40 x 48 inches
The Fleischer Museum, Scottsdale, Arizona

WHAT DID THE TSURAI, the local Yurok people, see 500 years ago when they gazed down the coastline from this remote seaside bluff? These great boulders, which they called Rtskrgr'n, were here then, of course—oversized shards from some moon-fallen sculpture, resting on a terrestrial sea of sand. Me'tsko, the little river, may have followed a slightly different course — must certainly have shimmered with the backs of steelhead!—but it took to the sea right here then, too. And further to the south of Me'tsko, the miles upon miles of beach were worked by the same surf, even if the expanse, extending to the limit of sight, was only visible when the fog lifted to reveal the cause of the constant roar. And when the Tsurai children gathered wild strawberries from Okwe'ges—the sand dunes—their voices must have carried up the flank of the bluff on these same warm currents of air.

Did those people, too, sit on these boulders and stare out to sea for the setting of the sun, or look up with wonder at the streaks of light in the nighttime sky?

None of this has changed, yet the coastline is not quite the same. Where the vast ocean at last laps against the sandy shores of this continent, we greet it with the scars of off-road tire tracks and the trace elements of the combustion engine. Tranquility is interrupted as engines roar, spinning tires spit sand, and masses of metal are propelled in every direction except the right one—toward roadways, away from this native coastline.

But, come winter, the river will rise, the storms will surge, and the surf will wash the sand slate clean: nature's way of erasing our mistakes.

GORDON HULL, *mead brewer*

worked with a neighboring rancher, I.D. Christensen, to post, fence, and patrol their land to keep out trespassers and off-road vehicles.

The Lanphere and Christensen properties include a coastal dune system where southern and northern flora overlap. Walking the sand hills, you might find tundra vegetation like reindeer lichen and bearberry interspersed with wild strawberry and manzanita. The dunes here also harbor rare plants such as Humboldt Bay wallflower, Humboldt Bay owl's clover, and beach layia. In 1974, The Nature Conservancy obtained an easement on the Lanphere property and purchased a portion of the adjoining Christensen property. Over the years, the Conservancy

Eugen Neuhaus (1879-1963)
Mouth of the Navarro, Mendocino, California
tempera on canvas, 24-1/8 x 20-1/8 inches
Courtesy of the Garzoli Gallery, San Rafael

Noyo River Country

CALIFORNIA IS A PARADOX. It is, from one perspective, one of the most highly engineered portions of the planet outside of the island of Manhattan. Its vast multi-billion-dollar water system, built across a century, moves water across the state with efficiency surpassing the aqueducts of Ancient Rome. Great bridges span San Francisco Bay, and the freeway system of California is universally considered one of the engineering marvels of the world. California is also a dense place in terms of its human habitation. With more than ninety-six percent of its population living in urban, suburban, or small town circumstances, California is among the most dense of American states as far as human settlement is concerned.

And yet, this state of bridges, freeways, aqueducts, dams, reservoirs, and population density takes nature as its primary symbol. As early as 1860, in fact, some sixty years before the National Park movement, Californians set aside the Yosemite as a wilderness preserve. The Sierra Club was founded here; and the great writers of California—Jack London, Frank Norris, Mary Austin, Robinson Jeffers and Gary Synder come immediately to mind—have always responded to nature as the matrix and primary theme of their writings. No state, with the possible exception of New York, can show such a profound and continuous engagement between artists and the environment as can California, whose history of painting and the fine arts begins with the Gold Rush itself.

To be a Californian, then, is to balance dualities of wilderness and human settlement, nature and technology, urbanism and the outdoors. Any tried and true Californian, whether a Californian by birth or by choice, exists on the cutting edge of this paradox: this dramatic interplay of urban/technocratic and environmental value. Each Californian, in fact, tends to have his or her special place: a portion of California, that is, that speaks directly to an internalized, imaginative sense of what California is in its best identity. Because the state is so varied, these special Californias can be found in the desert, in the mountains, in the Coast Ranges, in the great valleys of the interior, in the high plateaus of the northeast. Quite frequently, where Californians manage to have their second home, or where they manage to be for a portion of each year, usually at vacation time, bespeaks the exact location, texture, and coloration of their special California.

In some cases, such as my own, that special California place is anchored in the memories of childhood. For me, the coastal forest between Willits and Fort Bragg crossing through the Noyo River will always retain a certain intensity and personal significance. Served by the one-car trains of the California Western Railroad, Noyo River country is not, perhaps, as yieldingly beautiful as the Napa Valley, or as dramatic as the high desert, or as grand as the Sierra Nevada, or as planetary as Lake Tahoe. The mountains are small and somewhat huddled, and the Noyo River itself is among the less pretentious of our California waterways. Yet, I remember from my boyhood what it was like to hike through these mountains: to remerge from the forest into an open pear orchard, cleared of its trees in the frontier era. In later years, as a graduate student at Harvard, I came to see parallels between the Noyo River country of California and the hills of New Hampshire and Vermont. There was that similar intimacy: that sense of the mountains not overwhelming one, as do the mountains of the Sierra Nevada, but inviting to a more intimate relationship.

To this day, the country I am talking about—the forest and river country between Willits and Fort Bragg—remains relatively unsettled and obscure and manages to convey not only the mood of the nineteenth century frontier, but those similarities between New England and the north coast of California which are also reflected in the surviving nineteenth century and turn-of-the-century buildings of Fort Bragg, Mendocino, and the coastal towns further north.

DR. KEVIN STARR, State Librarian of California

expanded its holdings to include a salt marsh and other dune properties that had been damaged by off-road vehicles. In 1998, after years of work to eradicate invasive plant species in the newer properties, The Nature Conservancy transferred the Lanphere-Christensen Dunes Preserve to the U.S. Fish and Wildlife Service.

Just south of Mendocino, The Nature Conservancy has helped to preserve a biological phenomenon, a pygmy forest. Five wave-cut terraces of land rise from the Mendocino coast, the result of changing sea levels during the Ice Age. On the highest of these terraces, a layer of subsoil clay hinders drainage. Over the years, pooling water has leached most nutrients from the soil, severely stunting all vegetation. Pines that might grow 100 feet tall elsewhere attain elfin heights of eight feet here. Fifty-year-old cypresses rarely reach above your waist. Even huckleberry bushes and parasitic mistletoe grow as dwarves. The Nature Conservancy manages the pygmy forest in cooperation with the University of California Natural Reserve System and the California Department of Parks and Recreation.

In Lake County, The Nature Conservancy saved one of the largest, most distinctive vernal pools in the state. When Boggs Lake faced the prospect of being developed, the California Native Plant Society convinced the Conservancy to acquire the property because it supports a wealth of plant species found almost nowhere else in the world, including hedge hyssop, many-flowered navarretia, few-flowered navarretia, and Howell's dodder. The concentration of unusual species results from the fact that most vernal pools are situated in grasslands on sedimentary soil, while Boggs Lake has formed on a volcanic setting in the middle of a forest.

When people think of California, they often envision the type of wild landscapes common throughout the North Coast—lonely seascapes or cathedral redwood groves. But wildlands like these do more than serve as symbols of the California lifestyle. Their resources—fish, lumber, water—yield quantifiable value, as do the tourists who flock here to enjoy them. Untamed lands deliver intangible benefits, too. They sustain innumerable rare plants and animals, and, perhaps as important, they nourish human souls, providing interludes of quiet and solitude in a state where those experiences are becoming as endangered as many vanishing species. With its soaring population, California will surely lose some of its remaining wildlands, but dedicated and visionary organizations like The Nature Conservancy are working to secure many of those landscapes, so future generations can always enjoy California's native grandeur.

AFTERWORD

California, the Earthly Paradise

BY JOAN IRVINE SMITH

IT IS ALMOST UNIVERSALLY AGREED THAT HUMAN BEINGS ENTERED North America from Asia, over a land bridge that was exposed during an ice age across the present-day Bering Strait. The date that these people first crossed into North America is not generally agreed upon, but over the last few years, archaeological investigations have steadily pushed that date farther back into antiquity, possibly as long ago as 50,000 years or more before the present era.

The people who first populated North America were nomadic groups who obtained food by fishing and hunting, and by gathering fruits, nuts, berries, roots, and leaves of edible plants along their annual migration routes. They lived off the land, taking only what they could readily use before moving to a new area. In this manner, the land recovered quickly, and thus rejuvenated, would provide more sustenance for all living creatures that made up the local ecology.

In time, the people of what is now called the New World spread south and populated the entire Western Hemisphere, establishing remarkably advanced civilizations in Mesoamerica and on the Andean Plateau.

European presence in the New World began, of course, after 1492, the year that Christopher Columbus became the European discoverer of North America. Thereafter, Spanish expeditions successfully established bases, at first on the islands in the Caribbean Sea, and using these as stepping-stones, later on the mainland. These military expeditions were driven by the incentive of finding new sources of wealth, but at the same time, they were justified by what was believed to be a sacred duty: to systematically convert the native inhabitants to Christianity.

The first significant European entry in the North American mainland occurred in 1519, when Hernán Cortez set out to conquer the Aztec Empire in what is now Mexico. For many years, Spanish explorers believed Baja California to be the southern tip of a large island, an island they called "California," after a mythical land mentioned in a novel by Garcí Ordoñez de Montalvo. This book, *Las Segas de Esplandian*, (The Exploits of Esplandian) was written in 1510, many years before the discovery of California, and it

Arthur F. Mathews (1860-1945)
Discovery of San Francisco Bay by Portolá
oil on canvas, 70-1/4 x 58-1/2 inches
Courtesy of the Garzoli Gallery, San Rafael

proclaimed that a beautiful black Amazon queen named "Calafía" ruled a kingdom "on the right-hand side of the Indies, . . .which *was very close to the earthly paradise.*" As the Spanish explorers mistook Baja California to be an island and it was on the right-hand side of the Indies, so then they believed they had found "California."

Thereafter, driven by tales of fantastic wealth in the American Southwest, one expedition after another went in search of gold and jewels. In time, Spain realized that there was no great source of wealth in the Southwest, and the search was abandoned. Instead, Spain concentrated on the conquest of the Inca Empire throughout South America, and all further attempts to colonize North America were scaled down and ended in the early 1600s. Ironically, the Spanish explorers never realized that they had unknowingly overlooked one of the richest gold deposits ever known, a bonanza which would not be discovered until 1848.

It was not until 1769, by edict of King Carlos III, that Spain established permanent colonies in California. The catalyst for his abrupt change, of course, was apprehension that the Russian Empire was expanding into California from colonies in Alaska and the Pacific Northwest. Spanish colonization of California consisted of the establishment of *missions*, military forts called *presidios*, and small agricultural towns called *pueblos*. The sites that were chosen for these settlements had to meet certain requirements, the most important of which was an adequate supply of water. The task of setting up the missions fell to Father Junípero Serra and the presidios to Gaspár de Portolá, the Spanish Governor of Baja California.

In June 1769, Portolá led an expedition from Loreto, in Baja California, to San Diego, in Alta California, where Father Serra founded the Mission San Diego de Alcalá, the first in a series of twenty-one missions that would reach as far north as Sonoma. The Portolá Expedition was to scout, identify, and map potential sites for construction of the missions. They charted a series of locations throughout California, going as far north as present-day San Francisco.

On this journey, Portolá and his chief scout, Sergeant José Francisco Ortega, passed through a remarkably rich and diverse environment, a true "earthly paradise" inhabited by gentle and docile people. The expedition encountered endless vistas of rolling, grassy plains, verdant hills covered with extensive timber, and ranges of snow-covered mountains. The land contained a myriad of wild game including antelope, deer, and bear, as well as birds and waterfowl of all kinds. The lakes, rivers and coastal waters were full of fish and shellfish. They had come upon a temperate, hospitable land with seemingly endless sustenance, all theirs for the taking.

The Indians of California lived in harmony with the land, relying on the bountiful natural environment for all their food. This natural food supply was so abundant and diverse that California supported a native population far greater than any equal area in the United States. Except for a few tribes that practiced agriculture along the Colorado River, they lived entirely by hunting, fishing, and gathering. The great staple was the acorn, which has a higher caloric value than wheat, and when ground into flour and washed free of tannic acid, was made into porridge or bread.

The natural environment also provided all their material necessities, although they did not have the horse or the wheel. While they made the finest baskets in the United States, pottery is essentially absent in California, with the notable exception of some southern and desert areas. While they had no metal tools, they were experts at chipping stone and the items they made, points, blades, and scrapers, are among the most beautiful stone tools known.

The Spanish Empire was built and financed by exploiting the seemingly inexhaustible supply of colonial lands and natural resources, which, under Spanish law, was at the sole disposition of the king. In distant provinces, such as California, the presidios, pueblos, and missions, which Spain established for the conquest of the frontier, were all supported by royal concessions. Presidios and pueblos were permanent settlements, and in keeping with general laws, their lands were granted outright. The missions however, were expected to complete their tasks in about ten years, and then to transfer their holdings to the neophyte Indian converts. As such, they received only temporary rights, which could be cancelled at any time.

All California mission grants were of enormous size. To ensure the missions had all they needed for their important tasks, the king granted them very generous amounts of land. The largest of all was the Mission San Gabriel, which held land that stretched from the Arroyo Seco to the southwest, some fifteen miles to San Pedro, and to the east and southeast for fifty-two miles. In addition to pastureland, Mission San Gabriel held 6,000 acres of irrigated land for various crops to support its large neophyte population.

By the early 1830s, the peak period of the missions just prior to secularization, the twenty-one missions in Alta California, arranged along the 700 miles of El Camino Real, housed over 30,000 Indian neophytes. As a group, they kept more than 400,000 cattle, 60,000 horses, and 300,000 sheep, goats, and pigs. Their combined annual agricultural production totaled 120,000 bushels of wheat, corn, and beans. As for manufacturing, the mission system turned out substantial quantities of wine and brandy; hides for saddles and other leather goods; tallow which was made into soap and candles; olives and olive oil; wool for rough cloth; as well as cotton, hemp, linen, brick, tiles, tobacco, and salt.

Starting in the early 1800s, Spain began to encourage private development of land in California by issuing land grants. The large blocks of land, ranging from about 17,000 acres up to 50,000 acres, were given to people who were in a position to make proper use of the land, as farmland and ranchland. As vast as some of the ranchos were, they were not regarded as too large for ranching, where a dozen acres of grassland might be required to pasture a single cow through the long, dry summer season.

From the earliest days of colonization, Spanish authorities passed stringent laws designed to keep foreigners out of California. By the late 1700s, however, New England merchants discovered that there was a lucrative market in China for fur of the sea otter, which flourished along the Pacific coast from the Aleutian Islands to Baja California and particularly along the Alta California shores. The skin of a full-grown sea otter, when shipped to the Chinese port of Canton, brought the princely sum of about $300. Although the fur seal was more numerous, its pelt was less valuable.

By the end of the Spanish period, both the sea otter and the fur seal had become almost extinct along the coast of California. Although New England whalers began to visit the region more frequently, the main American trading interest on the coast shifted to cowhides and tallow. Hides, valued at about $2 a piece, were in fact the province's main form of currency and would eventually be called "California Bank Notes."

By the early 1820s, beaver fur became fashionable. At the time, the northern part of the Spanish province of Alta California had a thriving population of beaver, particularly in the San Joaquin and Sacramento rivers and their tributaries, and in the marshy areas of San Francisco Bay.

Just as American sea-going commerce with California had begun with the search for the sea otter, so the history of overland contact began with the quest for the beaver. Trappers were the spearhead of American landward advance, particularly in the far west, where they came over the Rocky Mountains, following their quarry from one stream to another.

The first American overland expedition to California in search of beaver was led by the fur trapper Jedediah Strong Smith (1799-1831) in 1826. As the first recorded white man to enter California by crossing the Rocky Mountains from the east, Smith well deserved the title of "The Pathfinder," a recognition bestowed years later upon the more publicized, but perhaps less-deserving, hero John C. Frémont.

Smith's long journey from Utah to the Mission San Gabriel proved that California could be reached by crossing the mountains. News of Smith's travels prompted others to do the same and eventually routes developed by Smith, Kit Carson, Joseph Walker, and others would open California to a large number of American immigrants. To the Mexican authorities, however, Smith's exploits were a serious threat as they proved that California's eastern frontier was no longer impassable.

During the Spanish Regime, ending in 1821, and for the first ten or twelve years of Mexican rule, about twenty private rancho grants were made in all of California. When the missions were secularized, starting in 1834, their vast acreage of field crops, vineyards, orchards, and pasture was now in the public domain, with some of it destined to be

William Wendt (1865-1946)
San Juan Creek
near the Mission
oil on canvas, 30 x 36 inches
Private collection, courtesy of
The Irvine Museum

divided among the Indians who were once part of the mission system. Within a few years, however, none of the land remained in Indian hands and nearly all of it was available for land grants at the discretion of the governor and other officials. It is not surprising that from 1834 to 1846, when California became an American possession, about 500 grants were made, most of which went to relatives or business associates of those public officials. Except for a few grants in the Sacramento Valley held mainly by naturalized foreigners like John Augustus Sutter, the ranchos of the "Golden Age," between 1834 and 1845, were located where the missions had been, in a narrow strip along the coast.

On the typical California rancho, there were between twenty and several hundred Indian workers. This work force included former mission Indians and new recruits gathered by the *ranchero* or ranch owner. In return for their labor, the Indians usually received nothing more than shelter, food, and clothing. Although the Indian laborers were legally free, they could not leave their employment if they were in debt to the ranchero, a state of dependency that was never allowed to end. In practice, the Indians were bound to the ranchero in a state of peonage. Rancho society was essentially feudal.

Throughout the Mexican period, the most substantial economic activity was cattle raising, and all other resources of California remained undeveloped. The only commercial products of this industry were hides and tallow, which were used almost exclusively for export and represented the sole source of profit for the ranchos.

The classic description of the hide and tallow trade was written by Richard Henry Dana in *Two Years Before the Mast*, published in 1840. Though it is usually thought of as a portrayal of life at sea and as a tract intended to reform the working conditions of seamen, much of the book was devoted to Dana's observations ashore in California.

When Dana left Boston harbor at age nineteen on the ship *Pilgrim* in 1834, the outward-bound cargo of "everything under the sun," was quickly disposed of at Monterey. There, boatloads of eager purchasers were rowed out to the ship, as if it was a floating department store, where they happily traded their hides and tallow for wide selection of manufactured goods.

The hide and tallow trade was significant not only because it influenced the economic history of New England and of early California, but also because, for many years, it increased interest of Americans in a distant region with which it formed almost their only contact. *Two Years Before the Mast* taught Americans the message, "In the hands of an enterprising people, what a country this might be!"

The missions, for their own use, had made such things as coarse woolen blankets, crude shoes, the leather parts of saddles, soap, candles, and crude pottery. They had also developed irrigated agriculture to the point of producing a remarkable variety of grains, vegetables, and fruits, and some wine and brandy.

After the missions were secularized, there was virtually no manufacturing. Nearly all consumer items were imported. Even such ordinary articles as brooms, soap, candles, tools, axes, dishes, knives and forks, soft cloth for clothing, wine, rum, tobacco, coffee, sugar, and salt, now came from abroad. Though California produced a great quantity of leather, very little was used locally. The manufacture of hides into shoes and other leather products was done in New England and later exported back to California. Even the simple processes of making soap and candles out of tallow were done in Chile or Peru.

In contrast to those who came to California only to exploit the fur trade, many American immigrants from 1821 to 1845 became citizens of Mexico, acquired land, opened stores, and built comfortable fortunes. One of the most famous of these was Johann Augustus Sutter (1803-1880), a German-Swiss who left his homeland, as well as his wife and children, to avoid going to debtor's prison.

He worked at various jobs in the United States before joining an American Fur Company party to the Rocky Mountains, in the spring of 1838. In Oregon, he had heard of the Sacramento Valley, and there, he now sought the wide-open spaces where people could plan things as they would like them to be. Wishing to reach California, he continued north to Vancouver, where he boarded a Hudson's Bay Company ship for Hawaii. From Hawaii, he took a merchant ship to California, arriving in Monterey on July 3, 1839, with his ambitious design for the Sacramento Valley.

Passing himself off as a Captain in the Swiss Guards, Sutter petitioned Governor Alvarado for a grant to start a settlement on 50,000 acres where the Sacramento and American rivers came together, in what is now the city of Sacramento. The land came with a stipulation to build a fort for the specific purpose of protecting California from raids by hostile Indians and controlling "American criminal elements," specifically trappers who were illegally entering California.

Sutter called his settlement *Nova Helvetia* (New Switzerland), but most people knew it simply as Sutter's Fort. From trading beaver pelts and wild grape brandy, Sutter went on to establish a cattle ranch and farm, using Indians and itinerant foreigners as laborers. He hired a German military drill instructor to train his Indian scouts. They obeyed orders implicitly and were often seen marching in goose-step around the parade grounds.

As the terminus of the emigrant trail from Missouri and an important frontier out-post, Sutter's Fort was to play a significant role in the history of the American movement overland into California. Even though he was commissioned to stem the flow of immi-grants, he actually encouraged it, and Sutter's Fort became a resting place for travelers who had made the perilous crossing over the Sierra Nevada Mountains, most notable of which were the forty-five survivors of the ill-fated Donner Party, in 1847.

On May 9, 1846, the United States declared war on Mexico. However, before news of the war could reach California, a group of armed American settlers took matters into

Paul Grimm (1892-1974)
Country Road
oil on canvas, 20 x 16 inches
Joan Irvine Smith Collection

their own hands and started the Bear Flag Rebellion by descending upon the village of Sonoma on June 14. They declared California a republic and devised a flag made of white cotton cloth with a star, a stripe, a grizzly bear, and "California Republic" lettered in black ink. This was the original of the banner the California legislature adopted in 1911 as the state flag. Lieutenant John C. Frémont, who was in California with a small detachment of troops ostensibly for scientific exploration, merged his forces with the "Bear Flaggers" and marched on the presidio at San Francisco.

With the Mexican War underway, the U. S. Navy moved to consolidate its position in California. On July 2, the United States Pacific Fleet, under the command of Commodore John Sloat, landed at Monterey. The *Californios* put up no resistance to the overwhelming might of the U.S. Navy. On July 7, Sloat officially hoisted the American flag, stating that "henceforth, California will be a portion of the United States."

The Mexican War ended with the Treaty of Guadalupe Hidalgo, in 1848. California, along with the entire American Southwest, became an American possession. One of the provisions of the treaty was an agreement that all Mexican land grants to the ranchos would be respected. Unfortunately, many of the old land grants had been improperly surveyed, and numerous boundary disputes arose. New American arrivals staked claims in large numbers on parts of undeveloped rancho lands. Only a few old families were able to preserve their ranchos. For most of the Californios, their lands and wealth slowly disappeared as they were forced to pay for legal services fighting to defend their land grants.

By late 1847, John Sutter's holdings had grown considerably. Among his many ventures was a partnership with James W. Marshall (1810-1885), a carpenter, to build and operate a saw mill on the American River. The region was quickly developing, and there was a great demand for lumber. Needing workmen to build the mill, Sutter hired veterans from the Mormon Battalion, men from the Midwest who had arrived in San Diego just after the fighting had ceased.

Construction of the mill required carpenters, who cut and assembled the lumber, and ordinary laborers, who dug a series of spillways to direct the flow of water. On January 24, 1848, when Marshall inspected the work, he found small flakes of gold in the banks of the river. Sutter tried to keep the discovery secret for several weeks while he acquired as much of the surrounding land as he could.

As soon as work on the mill was completed, the Mormons began prospecting in the vicinity of the mill and found substantial amounts of gold. They wrote home, telling of the gold strike, and soon, friends and relatives from Utah were in California, looking for gold on Sutter's land.

By May of 1848, the secret was out and most of the towns in the area were deserted as people took to the hills and valleys of the American River. By June, news of the gold strike was printed in San Francisco newspapers, and Sutter's property on the Sacramento

River was overrun by thousands of people hoping to find a fortune in gold. Squatters and businessmen set up tents and later cabins, and the city of Sacramento was born. By July, those same newspapers in San Francisco had to stop publication because most of their employees, as well as their readers, had gone to the gold fields.

News of the discovery began spreading outside California. At first, the stories of the gold strike were discounted as merely fantasy and rumors. It was not until the end of 1848, when President Polk gave his annual speech in Congress and actual examples of the rich gold nuggets were displayed in the east, that people throughout the country began to leave for California.

It is estimated that about 6,000 to 10,000 people came looking for gold in 1848. In 1849, that number swelled to more than 100,000, almost all of which were adult males. Immediately, Sutter's land was overrun by thousands of miners, who dug pits and shafts along the streams, cut down large numbers of trees for firewood and set up camps without regards for property rights, be they whites' or Indians'. In the end, the Gold Rush proved a financial disaster for Sutter. The Industrial Age had come to California, sounding the death-knell of the Agricultural Arcadia of bygone days.

The completion of the Transcontinental Railroad, at Promontory Point, Utah, in 1869, forged the first direct link from the east to California and opened the flood gates to large scale immigration in northern California. As this route terminated at Oakland, California, across the bay from San Francisco, however, it bypassed the potentially rich agricultural lands of southern California. In 1876, the Southern Pacific Railroad built a line from San Francisco south into Los Angeles. Meanwhile, the competing Santa Fe Railway extended a line from Missouri into the Southwest, past Santa Fe, and into Los Angeles by way of the Cajon Pass, in 1885. The line was later extended south to San Diego.

The County of Los Angeles, which, prior to 1889, included present-day Orange County, had almost 34,000 residents in 1880. By 1900, the two counties combined had a population of over 190,000 people, which dramatically increased to a figure well over 500,000 by 1910.

Although the great romantic image of Old California remains, the unique landscape has changed dramatically. The same environment that fills us with wonder is an important part of the quality of life that attracts millions of residents to the state. California is now home to more than 36 million people — one out of every eight persons in the United States. Reasonable estimates expect another 18 million citizens to call the state home by the year 2025, and we can also reasonably expect most of this population increase to take place in southern California.

Today, nearly 500 years after Spanish explorers first set foot on the west coast of the New World, looking for its mythical source of wealth, we now understand California's true "gold" lies in her beautiful and fragile environment that is indeed so ". . .very close to the earthly Paradise."

SOURCES

BLOMQUIST, WILLIAM, *Dividing the Waters: Governing Groundwater in Southern California*, The Center for Self Governance, ICS Press, San Francisco, California, 1992.

CLELAND, ROBERT GLASS, *The Irvine Ranch*, The Huntington Library, San Marino, California, 1952.

HALLAN-GIBSON, PAMELA, *Two Hundred Years in San Juan Capistrano*, The Donning Company, Norfolk, Virginia, 1990.

RAWLS, JAMES J., *California: An Interpretive History*, McGraw Hill, New York City.

SLEEPER, JIM, *Bears to Briquets, A History of Irvine Park, 1897–1997*, California Classics, Trabuco Canyon, California, 1997.

WALKER, DORIS I., *Dana Point Harbor / Capistrano Bay: Home Port for Romance*, To-The-Point Press, Dana Point, California, 1995.

Landscape Painting in California

BY JEAN STERN, *Executive Director, The Irvine Museum*

LANDSCAPE PAINTING IS AN INTEGRAL ASPECT OF American art. Indeed, from the earliest times, American art has been determined by unique circumstances. Unlike in many European countries, art in America was nurtured in the absence of patronage by the church or the monarchy, both of which were powerful determinants in the progress of European art. Instead, American artists preferred to paint landscapes and genre scenes, that is to say, paintings that show the everyday character of American life.

Inevitably, landscape painting became the ideal vehicle for expressing the American spirit, as it created a metaphor of the American landscape as the fountainhead from which sprang the bounty and opportunity of rustic American life. Moreover, landscape painting afforded an avenue to express God and Nature as one, an understanding of spirituality that disavowed official religious patronage. When America emerged on the world stage in the mid-nineteenth century, it was with an art tradition that reflected what was paramount to American society: its people and its land.

In keeping with this sincere and honest approach to American art, the artist resolved to paint as realistically as possible. The desire for realistic portrayal of forms has continually been a forceful characteristic of American art. In America, the search for truth in art expressed itself in a carefully observed and highly detailed manner associated with the artistic style called Realism. The convention of painting in a direct and truthful manner has persisted throughout the history of American art up to the present day, with only a few stylistic modifications.

Perhaps the most important and lasting influence on American art came from French Impressionism, in the latter part of the nineteenth century. Born in France in the late 1860s, Impressionism transformed French art. Reacting strongly against the artistic tenets of the French Academy, the Impressionists lamented the absence of spontaneity and the lack of natural light and color that often characterized an academic canvas, a consequence of painting exclusively in the studio and from posed models. They preferred instead to paint directly on primed canvas and to set the easel out-of-doors, to accurately capture light and atmospheric effects. Philosophically, they sought more relevance in subject matter, turning to everyday life for artistic motivation. They aspired for art that reflected the people as they were. Reluctant to pose a composition, Impressionists explored the fleeting moment or the "temporal fragment" of ordinary life.

Before the end of the decade, the persuasive energy of this new style was felt throughout Europe, and by the early 1890s, Impressionism was no longer uniquely French. Artists who had been art students in Paris in the 1880s, and who had seen firsthand what the style offered, were returning to their home countries. These young painters helped disseminate Impressionism to the rest of the world.

Whereas Impressionism made its debut amidst scorn and criticism in Paris, its arrival in the United States, sometime about 1885–1890, was relatively uneventful, and by the time it made its way to California, in the early 1890s, it had become an accepted part of American art. Clearly, it was a modified and toned-down rendering of the prototype French movement. Yet Impressionism changed American art in two ways: in the manner in which artists used color, and in the adoption of the distinct, loose brushwork that characterized the style. When one considers the resolute sense of realism that has always prevailed in American art, then perhaps the American experience with Impressionism would best be described as "Impressionistic Realism."

In America, artists of the mid-nineteenth century were keeping alive the tradition of realistic representation while, at the same time, scrutinizing all the influences from contemporary European art. A continent away, in California, artists were arriving in ever growing numbers to examine the aesthetic potential of this newly admitted state.

The Gold Rush had attracted large numbers of people to San Francisco, including many artists. They came for a variety of reasons: to profit from the economic boom, to find a new start, or simply to paint the scenic beauty of California. From the snow-capped peaks of the Sierra Nevada Mountains to the desolate splendor of the Mojave Desert; from the flower-covered coastal hills to the countless, secluded valleys; from the dazzling beaches of the south to the rocky coves of the north: the enthralling beauty of California is the principal reason that, from the middle of the 19th century on, painting in California has been characterized by a large number of light-filled landscape paintings.

Artists like Virgil Williams (1830-1886), William Keith (1839-1911) and Thomas Hill (1829-1908) were working in San Francisco as early as 1858. All three of these pivotal artists were trained in academic European styles and achieved maturity prior to the advent of Impressionism. They, and several other notable artists, who painted landscapes in a Romantic-Realist style closely associated with the French Barbizon school, came to characterize the art of northern California, and their students and followers continued in this style for many years. As such, they represented an entrenched artistic tradition that effectively inhibited the establishment of an Impressionist aesthetic in San Francisco until well after the turn of the 20th century. In consequence, young artists looking to settle in California in the late nineteenth century turned south.

Much has been offered about the desirability of the southern California climate, with its generous number of sunny days, as motivation for the advent of Impressionism in the south. Likewise, the San Francisco earthquake and fire of April 1906, caused a significant number of people, artists included, to move out of the city. Many San Francisco artists simply moved to Monterey and started an artists' colony on the scenic peninsula, but others continued south to Santa Barbara and Los Angeles. Whereas both factors exerted considerable influence, the chief motivation was surely economic opportunity, and Los Angeles, at the time not having a substantial artistic community, became the alternative metropolitan center that absorbed the infusion of young artists in California in the late 19th century.

In southern California, landscape painting was by far the most popular subject among painters, with nearly a complete absence of artists who painted urban scenes. Where the French Impressionists yearned to capture the immediate moment, or the "temporal fragment" of societal activity, California's Impressionists instead sought to catch the fleeting moment of specific natural light, as it bathed the landscape. In fact, light is the true subject of California Impressionists.

The clear and intense light of California, which appears so often in these paintings, defined the landscape. The biblical analogy of light as the creative instrument is appropriate to the manner in which the California Impressionists addressed the landscape, for without that unique light, and the divine energy it represented, the land would not exist.

Thus, the goal was to capture this striking visual sensation on canvas quickly, before the light changed. The key to achieving this goal was to get out of the studio and to paint outdoors, or *en plein air,* and to accentuate the role of color to produce brilliant light effects.

By 1895, several artists in Los Angeles were calling themselves Impressionist painters and painting in the plein-air approach. Benjamin C. Brown (1865-1942) was the most notable and influential of these. In the next decade, Granville Redmond (1871-1935), Hanson D. Puthuff (1875-1972), Marion Kavanagh Wachtel (1876-1954), William Wendt (1865-1946), and Franz A. Bischoff (1864-1929) would be added to the growing list of professional plein-air painters in southern California. Masters such as Jack Wilkinson Smith (1873-1949), Jean Mannheim (1863-1945), Maurice Braun (1877-1941), and Donna Schuster (1883-1953) moved to Los Angeles and became permanent residents by 1913. The following year, the illustrious Guy Rose (1867-1925) left France and returned to southern California, his homeland. Edgar Payne (1883-1947) and his wife, Elsie Palmer Payne (1884-1971) were making frequent visits to Los Angeles and Laguna Beach and settled permanently in 1917, and by the end of the decade, Alson S. Clark (1876-1949) and Joseph Kleitsch (1882-1931) had come to live in southern California.

At the end of the 1920s, the southern California art community experienced a series of dramatic transformations. A new generation of artists turned to new styles, characterized by a move away from the perceptual toward more conceptual approaches to painting. Furthermore, in 1929, the American economy suffered a terrible blow with the onset of the Great Depression. Almost overnight, the dynamic artist-dealer-patron relationship ground to a halt as much of America's disposable income vanished. The Depression was an indiscriminate misfortune to all artists. Modernists as well as plein-air artists joined in the Works Progress Administration programs, such as the Federal Arts Project, which allotted mural commissions in public buildings. Additionally, the American character turned inward and began a prolonged, restless period of self-examination. The arts followed suit and artists applied themselves to exploring the American experience in this time of solemnity. The bright, buoyant landscape paintings of the plein-air style were replaced with somber, comfortless views of the cities and the farms.

With economic recovery in the late 1930s, Modernism made its inroads, and by the outbreak of World War II, most of the prominent names of California Impressionism had died or had withdrawn from the public eye, and the style itself became a nostalgic souvenir of a bygone era.

Today, California plein-air painting has found a resurgence among landscape painters. From about 1980, the number of artists who choose to paint outdoors in the manner of their predecessors has increased dramatically. Under the leadership of Peter Adams, a nationally known plein-air painter, the California Art Club, an organization founded in 1909 by the original California Impressionists, is experiencing greater popularity than ever before in its long history. This Renaissance of the California Impressionist style coincides with society's growing awareness and concern for the natural environment. The Oak Group, founded in 1986 by landscape painters in the Santa Barbara area, partners with environmental organizations to donate half the proceeds from group plein-air shows to the defense of endangered lands. In northern California, a smaller group called the Baywood Artists has followed the same path, helping to preserve open space in the Bay Area.

It has been said that art is the most faithful statement that society can make about itself and that the mood and spiritual temperament of a people at a specific time and place is manifested in their art. If that is true, then the renewed artistic interest in praise of nature is good news for all of us.

Thanks and Acknowledgements

The publication of *Native Grandeur* was made possible by the vision and support of the Joan Irvine Smith and Athalie R. Clarke Foundation.

We would like to thank Elizabeth Brown, Monica Florian, Jim Lidberg, Cameron Barrows, and Ed Hastey, who all contributed to the research for this book.

We are grateful to many people for their advice and assistance in helping to select some of the paintings which illustrate the text. Joel Garzoli and John Garzoli at the Garzoli Gallery in San Rafael, Jessie Dunn-Gilbert, Barbara Janeff and Alfred Harrison at the North Point Gallery in San Francisco, Jean Stern at The Irvine Museum, and Harvey Jones at the Oakland Museum of California were very generous with their time and resources. We also thank Sara Beserra of *The Plein Air Scene*, Donna Fleischer of the Fleischer Museum in Scottsdale, Arizona, Dewitt Clinton McCall III of DeRu's Fine Arts in Laguna Beach, Ray Redfern of the Redfern Gallery in Laguna Beach, Zenaida Mott of the Baywood Artists, Daryn and Bill Horton, and Mary Welch.

Many thanks are also due to Julie Armistead at the Hearst Art Gallery in Moraga, Jeff Kramm and Claudia Kishler at the Oakland Museum of California, Megan Soske and Laura Benites at the Crocker Art Museum in Sacramento, Kristina Hornbeck at the Fresno Metropolitan Museum, Jeff Nickell at the Kern County Museum, Alicja Egbert at the Iris & B. Gerald Cantor Center for Visual Arts at Stanford University in Palo Alto, Mark and Colleen Hoffman at the Maxwell Gallery in San Francisco, and Lisa Peters at the Montgomery Gallery in San Francisco.

Finally, we thank the staff of The Nature Conservancy of California for their assistance with this book, and acknowledge with gratitude all of the conservation groups and private citizens whose work is chronicled in its pages.

DAVID WICINAS
LOUISA HUFSTADER
August 2000